SMARTER DIGITAL MARKETING WITH AI, MARTECH, AND AUTOMATION

A STEP-BY-STEP APPROACH TO IMPLEMENTING MODERN MARKETING TECHNOLOGIES IN EVERYDAY MARKETING

Rohit Srivastava

SMARTER DIGITAL MARKETING WITH AI, MARTECH, AND AUTOMATION

ISBN: 978-93-342-4148-8

LinkedIn: www.linkedin.com/in/rohitsrivastavas
Email: rohitkslko@gmail.com

DEDICATION

For my precious daughter, Prisha, and my son, Parth.

The light of my life and my greatest inspiration.

Your laughter fills my world with joy, and your endless curiosity reminds me to keep learning and growing every day.

With love and endless hope for your future, I hope this book serves as a small reminder that with passion, perseverance, and an open mind, you can achieve anything you dream of.

Your Father

Want to stay connected?

LinkedIn: www.linkedin.com/in/rohitsrivastavas
Email: rohitkslko@gmail.com

TABLE OF CONTENTS

PREFACE

Digital marketing is changing as new technologies become part of everyday work. In this book, the author offers a clear and practical look at how artificial intelligence, marketing technology, and automation can be incorporated into routine marketing practices.

Rather than promising dramatic results, the book presents a measured exploration of how these tools can support decision-making, improve efficiency, and help marketers understand their customers better.

The chapters are organized in a way that guides readers through the basics of digital marketing technology, the practical applications of AI, and the steps needed to integrate these tools into daily operations. The focus is on clear examples and real-world practices, so readers can see how the ideas discussed might work in their own work environments.

I appreciate that the author takes time to explain not only the potential benefits but also the challenges that come with adopting these technologies. By discussing topics like data quality, privacy, and the need for human oversight, the book offers a balanced perspective that is both informative and accessible.

For anyone looking to understand and apply these technologies in a straightforward way, this book serves as a practical guide. It encourages careful thought and deliberate action rather than relying on hype. I hope you find it useful in your journey as I have found it enlightening.

Rohit Srivastava

WHO THIS BOOK IS FOR

The world of digital marketing is undergoing a profound transformation. Artificial Intelligence (AI), Marketing Technology (MarTech), and automation are no longer futuristic concepts but integral components of modern marketing strategies. Whether you are a seasoned marketing professional, an entrepreneur, or someone new to the field, this book is designed to help you understand and leverage these technologies effectively.

Marketing Professionals Looking to Stay Ahead

If you are a marketing manager, strategist, or executive, you are likely already aware of how rapidly marketing is evolving. Traditional approaches are no longer sufficient to meet the expectations of today's digital consumers. This book will help you understand how AI and automation can improve your marketing campaigns, optimize performance, and improve customer engagement. You will gain insights into:

- How AI-driven analytics can refine your decision-making process.
- The role of automation in streamlining repetitive tasks and increasing efficiency.
- Personalization at scale and how AI can improve customer experiences.

Business Owners and Entrepreneurs

As a business owner or entrepreneur, you are constantly looking for ways to grow your business and remain competitive. AI and MarTech offer opportunities to optimize marketing strategies, improve customer acquisition, and refine engagement with minimal manual effort. This book will guide you through:

- The practical applications of AI and MarTech for small to medium-sized businesses.
- How automation can help scale operations without increasing overhead.
- Strategies to implement AI-driven marketing solutions cost-effectively.

Digital Marketers and Growth Hackers

If you specialize in digital marketing, SEO, or performance marketing, AI and MarTech are tools that can significantly boost your results. This book will explore:

- AI-powered customer segmentation and targeting techniques.
- Predictive analytics and how they can improve marketing performance.
- The impact of AI-driven content creation and optimization.

Marketing Technologists and Data Analysts

For those with a strong background in technology and data analysis, this book provides insights into the intersection of AI, data, and marketing. You will learn:

- How AI enhances data-driven decision-making processes.
- The role of machine learning in predictive analytics and performance measurement.
- How to integrate AI into existing marketing technology stacks.

Students and Aspiring Marketers

If you are a student or someone looking to transition into a marketing career, understanding AI and automation will give you a competitive advantage. This book will help you:

- Gain foundational knowledge of AI applications in marketing.

- Understand the evolution of MarTech and its role in digital marketing.
- Learn best practices for implementing AI-driven marketing strategies.

Tech Enthusiasts Interested in AI Applications

Even if you are not directly involved in marketing but have an interest in AI and its real-world applications, this book provides valuable insights into how AI is transforming a major industry. You will discover:

- Practical applications of AI beyond theoretical concepts.
- How businesses are using AI to solve real marketing challenges.
- Emerging trends in AI and MarTech are shaping the future of marketing.

Anyone Curious About the Future of Marketing

If you are simply curious about where marketing is headed and how AI and automation are shaping the industry, this book serves as a comprehensive guide. Whether you are a professional looking to upskill, a student preparing for the future, or a business owner wanting to stay competitive, this book provides actionable insights and practical strategies for leveraging AI, MarTech, and automation in digital marketing.

No matter what your background, this book is designed to be accessible, practical, and informative. By the end, you will have a clear understanding of how AI, MarTech, and automation are redefining marketing and how you can apply these technologies to achieve your marketing goals.

HOW TO USE THIS BOOK

The integration of AI, MarTech, and automation has reshaped digital marketing, providing businesses with tools to analyze data, optimize campaigns, and engage customers with greater precision. These technologies help marketers streamline operations, personalize customer experiences, and make informed decisions based on real-time insights.

While the benefits are clear, implementing AI-driven strategies require careful consideration of data quality, compliance regulations, and system integration. Businesses must balance automation with human oversight to ensure that marketing efforts remain strategic, creative, and customer centric.

As AI and automation continue to evolve, their role in marketing will expand, offering new opportunities to boost efficiency and improve engagement. Organizations that embrace these innovations with a thoughtful approach will be better positioned to adapt to changing consumer behaviors and market dynamics. By leveraging these tools effectively, businesses can create more meaningful connections with their audiences while maintaining agility in an increasingly digital world. Understand the concepts of each chapter to implement these strategies effectively.

INTRODUCTION

Digital marketing has steadily progressed, and today's marketing professionals are finding that new technologies such as artificial intelligence, marketing technology, and automation have become part of everyday work. This book offers a practical guide to understanding these tools and how they can be integrated into routine marketing practices.

The content here is organized to provide a clear overview of each technology, explain how they work together, and illustrate how they can be applied in various aspects of marketing—from customer segmentation and personalized content to data-driven decision-making and performance measurement. Rather than presenting these tools as a one-size-fits-all solution, the book addresses both the potential benefits and the challenges that come with adopting new technology.

As you progress through the chapters, you will encounter step-by-step approaches, real-world examples, and discussions of practical strategies. The goal is to offer you insight into how these technologies might be used in your work, while also considering issues such as data quality, privacy, and the importance of maintaining a human touch in marketing.

I hope that this book provides you with a clear, balanced view of modern digital marketing techniques and helps you decide how to best incorporate these technologies into your daily practices. Enjoy the journey as we explore a thoughtful and measured approach to a rapidly changing field.

PART I
FOUNDATIONS OF AI, MARTECH, AND AUTOMATION

MODULE 1
INTRODUCTION TO AI, MARTECH, AND AUTOMATION IN DIGITAL MARKETING

Digital marketing has undergone significant changes over the years, driven by technological advancements, changing consumer behaviors, and evolving market dynamics. Traditional marketing methods relied heavily on broad campaigns, where messaging was designed to appeal to a wide audience without granular targeting. However, the rise of digital channels introduced new ways to reach consumers, making marketing efforts more targeted and efficient.

With the increasing volume of digital interactions, businesses now rely on data to make informed marketing decisions. AI, marketing technology (MarTech), and automation play crucial roles in helping marketers analyze data, optimize campaigns, and improve customer experiences. These tools enable businesses to respond to changes in consumer behavior, personalize interactions, and maximize the effectiveness of their marketing efforts.

UNDERSTANDING AI, MARTECH, AND AUTOMATION

AI IN MARKETING

Artificial Intelligence (AI) in marketing refers to using machine learning algorithms, natural language processing, and data analytics to automate and improve various marketing functions. AI-powered systems can process vast amounts of data, identify patterns, and generate insights that help marketers refine their strategies. Some key applications of AI in marketing include:

Predictive Analytics | AI analyzes historical data to forecast trends and consumer behaviors. This allows marketers to anticipate demand, adjust inventory, and allocate budgets efficiently. Predictive analytics help businesses make informed decisions by identifying patterns in past consumer interactions. By leveraging these insights, companies can optimize product offerings, enhance customer targeting, and improve overall marketing performance. AI-driven predictive models can also help organizations mitigate risks, detect anomalies, and refine pricing strategies based on historical and real-time information.

Personalization | AI-driven algorithms tailor marketing messages, product recommendations, and advertisements based on user preferences and browsing behaviors. Personalization enables brands to deliver relevant content to specific audience segments, improving engagement and conversion rates. AI enhances personalization by analyzing past interactions, purchase history, and browsing patterns to curate experiences that align with individual preferences. Businesses use AI-powered recommendation engines to present personalized product suggestions, email campaigns, and dynamic website content, fostering stronger relationships with customers.

Chatbots and Virtual Assistants | AI-powered chatbots provide instant customer support, answer inquiries, and assist with transactions, improving the overall user experience. These digital assistants streamline customer service by handling routine queries, reducing response times, and enhancing accessibility. Chatbots can be programmed to understand natural language, provide personalized responses, and escalate complex issues to human agents when necessary. AI-driven virtual assistants are also integrated into voice-activated platforms, enabling users to interact with brands through conversational interfaces.

Content Optimization | AI tools analyze engagement metrics, such as click-through rates and time spent on pages, to optimize content strategies and ensure relevance to target audiences. AI-driven content optimization involves evaluating performance data, assessing audience preferences, and recommending improvements to maximize impact. Automated content generation tools assist marketers in creating blog posts, social media updates, and ad copies that align with consumer interests. AI can also boost search engine optimization (SEO) efforts by identifying relevant keywords, optimizing metadata, and predicting content trends.

Programmatic Advertising | AI automates the buying and placement of digital ads, ensuring that ads are displayed to the right audience at the right time. Programmatic advertising uses machine learning algorithms to analyze user behavior, bid in real-time auctions, and optimize ad placements across various channels. This approach enhances ad targeting precision, reduces wasted ad spend, and improves campaign efficiency. AI-powered programmatic platforms assess audience data, monitor ad performance, and adjust bidding strategies dynamically to achieve better return on investment (ROI).

MARKETING TECHNOLOGY (MarTech)

MarTech encompasses a wide range of tools and platforms that assist in managing, analyzing, and optimizing marketing efforts. These technologies streamline various processes, making it easier for marketers to execute campaigns effectively. Some core components of MarTech include:

Customer Relationship Management (CRM | CRM platforms store and manage customer interactions, helping businesses track leads, improve relationships, and personalize outreach efforts. These platforms help sales and marketing teams align their efforts by centralizing customer data, tracking communication history, and automating follow-ups. Businesses can segment customers based on demographics, purchase history, and engagement levels, allowing for more targeted marketing campaigns. Additionally, CRM software often integrates with email marketing tools, customer service platforms, and sales automation systems, enabling businesses to deliver consistent customer experience.

Marketing Automation Software | These tools automate repetitive tasks such as email marketing, social media posting, and lead nurturing, reducing manual effort while increasing efficiency. Marketing automation software allows businesses to schedule content distribution, track user interactions, and trigger follow-up communications based on customer behavior. By automating workflows, companies can maintain engagement with potential customers without requiring constant manual input. These platforms also offer analytics that help marketers refine their messaging and targeting strategies over time.

Data Analytics and Visualization Tools | Software that collects, organizes, and interprets data allows businesses to measure campaign performance and refine marketing strategies. These tools process vast amounts of structured and unstructured data to generate actionable insights. Businesses use analytics platforms to monitor customer engagement, website traffic, conversion rates, and advertising effectiveness. Visualization tools transform complex datasets into easy-to-understand dashboards and reports, enabling marketers to make informed decisions quickly.

Content Management Systems (CMS | CMS platforms enable marketers to create, manage, and distribute digital content seamlessly. These systems provide user-friendly interfaces that allow marketing teams to update website content, publish blog posts, and organize multimedia assets. Many CMS platforms support collaboration between content creators, designers, and SEO specialists, ensuring cohesive branding and optimized user experiences. Some CMS tools also incorporate AI-driven recommendations to improve content relevance and visibility.

Social Media Management Tools | These applications schedule posts, track engagement, and provide insights into audience behavior. Social media management tools help businesses maintain a consistent presence across multiple platforms by automating post scheduling and monitoring interactions. They also offer analytics on post performance, audience demographics, and engagement trends, allowing brands to refine their strategies. Many tools include sentiment analysis features, helping businesses gauge public perception and respond to customer feedback on time.

AUTOMATION IN DIGITAL MARKETING

Marketing automation refers to the use of software and AI-driven processes to execute repetitive marketing tasks with minimal human intervention. Automation allows marketers to focus on strategy while ensuring efficiency and consistency in execution. Key areas where automation plays a role include:

Email Campaigns | Automated workflows trigger personalized email responses based on user actions, such as abandoned carts or recent purchases. Email automation allows businesses to maintain consistent communication with customers while optimizing engagement through personalization. When a user abandons a shopping cart, automation tools can send a series of reminder emails, possibly including incentives like discounts or free shipping. Similarly, transactional emails, such as order confirmations and shipping notifications, can be enhanced with relevant product recommendations. Companies can use segmentation to ensure that email content is aligned with user preferences and behavior patterns. Advanced AI models analyze open rates, click-through rates, and conversions to refine subject lines, send times, and message content. As technology continues to evolve, businesses will likely integrate automation with predictive analytics to anticipate customer needs and offer proactive solutions.

Lead Scoring | AI assigns scores to potential customers based on their interactions, helping sales teams prioritize high-intent prospects. Lead scoring relies on data-driven algorithms that assess factors such as engagement levels, browsing behavior, and past purchase history to determine the likelihood of conversion. Businesses can assign values to different touchpoints, such as email interactions, website visits, or social media engagement, and generate a cumulative lead score. By prioritizing leads based on these scores, sales teams can allocate resources effectively, focusing on high-value prospects. AI enhances this process by continuously learning from new data and adjusting scoring criteria to improve accuracy. Companies also integrate lead scoring with marketing automation tools to trigger personalized outreach campaigns at optimal moments in the buyer's journey.

Ad Campaign Optimization | Automated tools analyze campaign performance and adjust bids, targeting, and creative elements to improve efficiency. Digital advertising platforms use AI-driven optimization techniques to refine audience targeting, ensuring that ads reach users who are most likely to engage. Machine learning models assess user behavior, contextual data, and conversion history to dynamically adjust bids in real time. By automating bid adjustments, marketers can allocate budgets efficiently and maximize return on investment. Additionally, ad creative elements, including headlines, images, and calls to action, can be A/B tested using AI tools, allowing marketers to refine messaging based on audience preferences. AI-powered insights also inform cross-channel strategies, enabling businesses to optimize campaign performance across multiple platforms such as social media, search engines, and display networks.

Customer Segmentation | Automation categorizes users based on their behaviors, demographics, and preferences, allowing for targeted messaging. Customer segmentation helps businesses tailor marketing efforts to different audience groups by analyzing user interactions, purchasing behavior, and demographic details. Segmentation strategies may include geographic, psychographic, behavioral, or value-based categorization. Automation enables real-time updates to segmentation criteria, ensuring that users receive relevant content based on their most recent interactions. AI enhances segmentation by identifying hidden patterns within datasets and creating micro-segments that improve personalization. Automated customer segmentation allows marketers to refine email marketing campaigns, adjust ad targeting, and deliver customized content experiences that align with user expectations. Businesses leveraging AI-powered segmentation can improve customer retention, boost engagement, and increase conversion rates by delivering highly relevant messaging at scale.

THE IMPORTANCE OF AI, MARTECH, AND AUTOMATION IN DIGITAL MARKETING

The integration of AI, MarTech, and automation into digital marketing strategies provides several advantages that help businesses achieve their marketing objectives.

Enhancing Efficiency

AI and automation reduce the time spent on manual tasks, such as data analysis, campaign execution, and performance tracking. Marketers can allocate more resources to strategic planning and creative development instead of repetitive processes. This efficiency leads to faster decision-making and more agile marketing execution.

Improving Personalization

Consumers expect personalized experiences when interacting with brands. AI-driven personalization allows marketers to tailor content, recommendations, and advertisements based on individual preferences. This level of customization leads to higher engagement rates and improved customer satisfaction.

Optimizing Decision-Making with Data

AI-powered analytics tools process large data sets to generate actionable insights. Marketers can make data-driven decisions regarding campaign adjustments, budget allocations, and content strategies. Predictive analytics further assists by forecasting customer behaviors, helping brands anticipate market changes.

Strengthening Customer Engagement

Chatbots, virtual assistants, and AI-powered support systems enhance customer interactions by providing quick responses and personalized assistance. These tools ensure that businesses remain available to customers around the clock, leading to improved satisfaction and retention.

CHALLENGES AND CONSIDERATIONS

While AI, MarTech, and automation offer significant benefits, they also present challenges that marketers must address for successful implementation.

Data Privacy and Compliance

As AI relies on data for decision-making, businesses must ensure compliance with data protection regulations such as GDPR and CCPA. Transparency in data collection and ethical handling of customer information are critical for maintaining trust.

Integration Complexity

Integrating AI and automation with existing marketing systems requires careful planning. Businesses must ensure that their tools work together seamlessly to avoid inefficiencies and data silos.

Dependence on Quality Data

AI models perform best when they have access to accurate and comprehensive data. Poor data quality can lead to incorrect predictions and ineffective marketing strategies. Businesses must invest in data management practices to maintain reliability.

Human Oversight and Strategy

Despite automation, human involvement remains essential in marketing. AI assists with analysis and execution, but strategic decision-making, creativity, and customer relationships require human expertise.

WHY AI, MARTECH, AND AUTOMATION ARE GAME CHANGERS

As technology continues to evolve, AI, MarTech, and automation will become even more integral to digital marketing. Some future trends include:

Advanced AI Models

AI is evolving to handle more complex data, refine personalization techniques, and automate decision-making, which contributes to improved marketing precision and efficiency.

Voice and Visual Search Integration

AI-driven progress in voice and visual search is making it more convenient for users to locate relevant products and services using non-text-based search inputs.

AI-Generated Content

AI-powered tools are facilitating scalable content generation, assisting marketers in producing material that aligns with audience preferences while maintaining relevance.

Automation continues to refine marketing operations across multiple digital platforms, ensuring that branding, messaging, and customer engagement remain cohesive and responsive.

Key Takeaways

- Digital marketing has evolved significantly, with AI, MarTech, and automation playing a key role in improving efficiency, personalization, and decision-making.
- AI-driven tools help marketers analyze data, optimize campaigns, and create personalized customer experiences.
- MarTech includes CRM platforms, marketing automation software, and data analytics tools that streamline marketing efforts.
- Automation simplifies repetitive marketing tasks, such as email campaigns, lead scoring, and ad optimization, allowing marketers to focus on strategy.
- While AI and automation offer significant advantages, businesses must address challenges such as data privacy, integration complexities, and the need for human oversight.

Reflection Questions

- How has your approach to digital marketing changed with the rise of AI and automation?
- Which aspects of AI or MarTech do you think would have the biggest impact on your current marketing strategy?
- What challenges do you foresee in integrating AI and automation into your business processes?
- How can you ensure that automation enhances personalization without losing the human touch in customer interactions?

Action Steps

- Identify one AI-driven tool or MarTech solution that could improve your marketing processes and research its potential benefits.
- Assess your current marketing efforts and determine which tasks could be automated to save time and improve efficiency.
- Review your data collection and management practices to ensure that they align with privacy regulations and best practices.
- Experiment with a small-scale automation tool (e.g., an AI-powered chatbot or automated email campaign) to test its effectiveness before full implementation.

MODULE 2
HOW MARKETING TECHNOLOGY HAS TRANSFORMED OVER TIME

Marketing has undergone a profound transformation over the past few decades, shifting from traditional methods to a more digitally driven approach. This evolution has been driven by technological advancements and changes in consumer behavior, requiring businesses to adapt to stay competitive.

Initially, marketing relied heavily on traditional channels such as print advertisements, billboards, radio broadcasts, and television commercials. These methods allowed companies to reach large audiences but lacked the ability to provide real-time feedback or measure consumer engagement effectively. Businesses depended on market research, surveys, and customer feedback to assess the impact of their campaigns, which often led to delayed adjustments in strategy.

With the rise of the internet, a new era of marketing began. Businesses started leveraging websites, email marketing, and digital advertisements to reach their target audiences more efficiently. Unlike traditional methods, digital marketing enabled real-time interactions and measurable results. Companies could now analyze customer behavior, track website traffic, and adjust their strategies accordingly.

The emergence of social media platforms further revolutionized marketing. Businesses gained direct access to consumers through platforms like Facebook, Twitter, LinkedIn, and Instagram. These channels facilitated two-way communication, allowing brands to engage with their audiences on a more personal level. Unlike traditional media, where messaging was one-way, social media encouraged interaction, feedback, and community-building.

THE ROLE OF TECHNOLOGY IN MODERN MARKETING

Marketing technology, commonly referred to as MarTech, encompasses a wide range of tools and software designed to optimize marketing efforts. As digital marketing gained prominence, businesses sought innovative solutions to enhance efficiency, improve targeting, and automate processes. Some key components of MarTech include:

Customer Relationship Management (CRM) Systems

These systems help businesses manage customer interactions, track leads, and maintain detailed customer profiles. CRM solutions enable companies to personalize their marketing efforts and nurture long-term relationships with their audience. They facilitate seamless communication between sales and marketing teams, ensuring that leads are effectively managed and converted into customers. Additionally, CRM tools provide insights into customer preferences, allowing businesses to create tailored marketing campaigns and improve retention rates. Modern CRMs integrate with other marketing technologies, enhancing automation and streamlining operations across various channels.

Marketing Automation Platforms

These tools allow businesses to schedule and execute campaigns across multiple channels, streamlining processes such as email marketing, social media posting, and lead nurturing. By automating repetitive tasks, marketing teams can focus on strategy and creative initiatives. Marketing automation platforms also offer advanced segmentation, enabling personalized messaging for different audience groups. They help businesses maintain consistent engagement with prospects and customers, ensuring that marketing efforts are both timely and relevant. Additionally, these platforms provide detailed analytics, helping marketers assess campaign performance and optimize future strategies.

Data Analytics and Business Intelligence

Marketers use data analytics tools to gain insights into consumer behavior, campaign performance, and market trends. These insights help refine marketing strategies and improve decision-making. With the ability to track key performance indicators (KPIs), businesses can evaluate the effectiveness of their marketing initiatives and make data-driven adjustments. Business intelligence tools integrate data from multiple sources, providing a comprehensive view of customer interactions. Predictive analytics further enhance marketing efforts by forecasting trends and identifying potential opportunities. Companies that leverage data analytics effectively can improve customer targeting, enhance engagement, and increase conversion rates.

Content Management Systems (CMS)

CMS platforms, such as WordPress and Drupal, enable businesses to create, manage, and distribute digital content efficiently. These platforms provide an intuitive interface for content creation, allowing marketers to publish blog posts, landing pages, and multimedia content without extensive technical knowledge. A well-structured CMS ensures consistent branding and messaging across digital channels. Additionally, CMS platforms support search engine optimization (SEO) strategies, improving website visibility and organic traffic. Many CMS solutions also integrate with analytics and marketing automation tools, facilitating data-driven content strategies that enhance user engagement and customer retention.

Advertising Technology (AdTech)

AdTech solutions improve ad targeting and performance measurement. They help marketers optimize ad placements, bidding strategies, and audience segmentation to maximize return on investment (ROI). Programmatic advertising, a key component of AdTech, uses AI-driven algorithms to automate ad buying and placement, ensuring that ads reach the most relevant audience at the right time. Real-time bidding (RTB) platforms further enhance efficiency by enabling advertisers to bid for ad space dynamically. AdTech also provides in-depth analytics, allowing businesses to track ad performance, measure engagement metrics, and refine their advertising strategies based on data-driven insights.

THE EMERGENCE OF AI IN MARKETING TECHNOLOGY

Artificial Intelligence (AI) has introduced new possibilities in marketing technology, enhancing personalization, predictive analytics, and automation. AI-driven solutions help businesses optimize their marketing strategies by analyzing large volumes of data and making real-time adjustments. Some notable applications of AI in marketing include:

Chatbots and Virtual Assistants

AI-powered chatbots provide real-time customer support, answering queries and assisting with purchasing decisions. These virtual assistants are designed to simulate human conversations and offer responses based on predefined scripts or machine-learning models. They enhance customer experience by providing immediate assistance, reducing response times, and handling multiple interactions simultaneously. Businesses implement chatbots on websites, messaging apps, and social media platforms to engage customers efficiently. Advanced AI-driven virtual assistants integrate with CRM systems, allowing them to provide personalized responses based on customer history. While chatbots streamline customer service, they also pose challenges, such as ensuring seamless human handoff for complex inquiries.

Predictive Analytics

AI algorithms process large datasets to identify patterns and trends, enabling businesses to forecast future consumer behavior. By analyzing historical data, predictive analytics help marketers anticipate customer needs and tailor their strategies accordingly. For example, e-commerce companies use predictive models to recommend products based on browsing and purchasing history. Additionally, predictive analytics enhance lead scoring, allowing sales teams to prioritize high-potential customers. However, successful implementation requires data accuracy, proper modeling, and continuous refinement to avoid biases. Ethical considerations, such as data privacy and transparency, also play a role in predictive analytics adoption.

AI-Powered Personalization

Personalization powered by AI leverages user data to tailor marketing content, product recommendations, and promotional messages. This approach enhances customer engagement by delivering relevant experiences based on individual preferences and behaviors. Retailers use AI-driven personalization engines to suggest products aligned with customer interests, while streaming platforms curate content recommendations based on viewing habits. Personalization extends to email marketing, where AI dynamically adjusts subject lines, content, and timing for maximum engagement. However, excessive personalization may raise concerns about data privacy and consumer trust. Striking a balance between relevance and ethical data usage is crucial for effective AI-driven personalization.

Automated Campaign Management

AI-driven automation optimizes advertising strategies by adjusting bids, targeting, and messaging in real-time. Marketers use AI-powered tools to manage campaigns across multiple platforms, ensuring ads reach the right audience at the right moment. Machine learning algorithms analyze performance data to refine audience segments and allocate budgets efficiently. Automated A/B testing helps marketers determine which creatives and messaging resonate best with users. Despite these advantages, automation requires human oversight to prevent misalignment with brand objectives. Businesses must also stay updated on evolving advertising regulations to ensure compliance with data protection laws.

KEY PHASES IN THE EVOLUTION OF MARKETING TECHNOLOGY

The Early Days Traditional Advertising and Direct Marketing

Before digital marketing, businesses relied on traditional advertising methods, including print media, radio, and television commercials. Direct marketing approaches, such as telemarketing and direct mail campaigns, were used to reach consumers directly. However, these strategies had limitations, including high costs and the inability to measure effectiveness in real-time.

The Digital Revolution in Websites, Email, and Search Engine Marketing

The rise of the internet in the 1990s marked a significant shift in marketing. Businesses began creating websites to establish an online presence. Email marketing emerged as an efficient way to communicate with customers directly, offering a cost-effective alternative to traditional direct mail.

Search engines like Google introduced pay-per-click (PPC)

advertising, enabling businesses to target users based on search queries. Search Engine Optimization (SEO) has become a crucial strategy, helping brands improve their visibility in search results and attract organic traffic.

Social Media and Mobile Marketing

The early 2000s saw the rapid growth of social media platforms, offering new opportunities for brands to engage with consumers. Businesses could now create content, interact with audiences, and run targeted ads on platforms like Facebook, Twitter, and Instagram.

Simultaneously, the widespread adoption of smartphones led to the rise of mobile marketing. Companies optimized their websites for mobile devices, developed mobile apps, and leveraged SMS marketing to connect with users on the go.

Big Data and Marketing Automation

With the expansion of digital marketing, businesses began collecting vast amounts of data from online interactions. Big Data analytics enabled companies to process and interpret this information, gaining deeper insights into customer behavior.

Marketing automation platforms became essential, allowing businesses to streamline their campaigns, segment audiences, and automate repetitive tasks. This phase marked a shift towards data-driven marketing strategies.

AI-Powered Marketing and Hyper-Personalization

Today, AI-driven marketing solutions enable hyper-personalization, where businesses can tailor content, product recommendations, and advertising to individual consumers in real-time. AI-powered tools analyze vast datasets to identify patterns, predict customer behavior, and optimize marketing campaigns.

THE BENEFITS OF MARKETING TECHNOLOGY

Efficiency and Automation

MarTech tools help businesses streamline their marketing efforts by automating repetitive tasks such as email campaigns, social media posting, and customer segmentation. Automation reduces manual effort, allowing marketing teams to allocate more time to strategic planning and creative execution. Additionally, automation tools improve workflow efficiency by integrating with customer relationship management (CRM) systems, ensuring seamless communication across departments. However, businesses must be mindful of over-automation, which can lead to impersonal customer experiences if not managed effectively.

Data-Driven Decision Making

Businesses rely on marketing analytics tools to gather data on customer behavior, campaign performance, and market trends. This data-driven approach allows organizations to measure the effectiveness of their strategies and make informed decisions. By analyzing key performance indicators (KPIs), businesses can identify which campaigns resonate with their audience and adjust their tactics accordingly. Predictive analytics also play a role in anticipating customer preferences and optimizing marketing messages. While data-driven marketing improves accuracy, companies must ensure data integrity and avoid misinterpretation that could lead to ineffective strategies.

Improved Customer Experience

AI-powered tools and automation enhance customer interactions by providing personalized and timely engagement. Chatbots and virtual assistants handle customer queries in real-time, ensuring faster response times and increased satisfaction. Personalized email marketing campaigns tailored to user behavior and preferences help create a more engaging experience. Businesses also use sentiment analysis tools to gauge customer opinions and improve service offerings. However, while technology enhances customer experience, companies should maintain a human touch to ensure that interactions remain authentic and empathetic.

Enhanced Targeting and Reach

Digital marketing tools enable precise audience segmentation based on demographic, geographic, and behavioral data. This capability allows businesses to target specific customer groups with tailored messages, improving conversion rates and reducing wasted ad spend. Social media platforms and programmatic advertising utilize machine learning to refine audience targeting and deliver relevant content to users. Businesses can also track user engagement metrics to optimize campaigns continuously. Despite these advantages, marketers should balance personalization with consumer privacy concerns, ensuring compliance with data protection regulations.

CHALLENGES IN ADOPTING MARKETING TECHNOLOGY

Integration with Existing Systems

Businesses often struggle with integrating new MarTech solutions with their legacy systems. This challenge arises due to outdated infrastructure, data silos, and compatibility issues between different technologies. Effective integration requires careful planning, a phased implementation approach, and sometimes, custom API development to facilitate seamless data exchange. Companies must also ensure proper training for employees to handle the transition smoothly and prevent workflow disruptions.

Data Privacy and Compliance

As businesses collect and analyze vast amounts of customer data, they must comply with data protection regulations such as the General Data Protection Regulation (GDPR) and other applicable laws. Organizations need to implement stringent data governance policies, obtain explicit user consent, and ensure secure data storage practices. Failure to adhere to these regulations can lead to legal consequences and reputational damage. Businesses should stay updated on evolving compliance requirements and adopt technologies that prioritize data security and ethical handling of consumer information.

Managing Complexity

The marketing technology landscape is continuously expanding, with numerous tools available for various functions. Selecting the right MarTech stack requires a strategic approach, considering factors such as business objectives, scalability, and integration capabilities. Many businesses face challenges in managing multiple platforms, ensuring interoperability, and preventing technology redundancies. To mitigate complexity, organizations should conduct regular MarTech audits, streamline workflows, and invest in training to maximize tool utilization.

Cost and ROI Measurement

Implementing and maintaining MarTech solutions requires financial investments, and businesses must assess the return on investment (ROI) to justify these expenditures. Many organizations struggle with accurately measuring the effectiveness of their marketing technologies. Establishing clear performance metrics, tracking key indicators such as customer acquisition costs and conversion rates, and using attribution models can help businesses evaluate their MarTech investments. Companies should also explore cost-effective solutions, leverage free trials, and periodically reassess their technology stack to optimize spending.

THE FUTURE OF MARKETING TECHNOLOGY

Looking ahead, marketing technology will continue to evolve with advancements in AI, automation, and data integration. Emerging trends include:

Voice Search Optimization | As voice-activated search queries become more prevalent, businesses will need to adapt their digital content to match the conversational nature of voice search. This includes optimizing keywords for natural language processing (NLP), improving website loading speeds, and ensuring mobile compatibility. Additionally, businesses must focus on featured snippets and structured data to increase the likelihood of appearing in voice search results. The integration of voice search with smart devices also presents new opportunities for marketing and advertising.

Blockchain in Digital Marketing | Blockchain technology has the potential to improve transparency and security in digital advertising by providing a decentralized ledger for tracking transactions. This could help reduce fraud in digital advertising by ensuring that advertisers only pay for genuine clicks and impressions. Blockchain also offers potential for enhancing data privacy, allowing users to control how their personal information is shared. Marketers may explore blockchain-based loyalty programs, which provide customers with verifiable and transferable rewards.

Augmented Reality (AR) and Virtual Reality (VR | AR and VR technologies offer businesses opportunities to create immersive marketing experiences. Retailers can allow customers to visualize products in real-world settings before making a purchase, while travel companies can offer virtual tours of destinations. Interactive brand experiences using AR and VR can improve engagement and lead to higher conversion rates. However, businesses will need to invest in the necessary infrastructure and content creation tools to effectively implement these technologies.

AI-Powered Content Generation | AI-driven tools are increasingly assisting in creating marketing content tailored to audience preferences. These tools analyze data to generate product descriptions, social media posts, and even long-form articles. AI can also help optimize content for SEO by identifying trending topics and relevant keywords. While AI-powered content generation improves efficiency, human oversight remains essential to ensure that content aligns with brand voice and quality standards.

The evolution of marketing technology has fundamentally changed how businesses interact with their audiences, shifting from broad traditional advertising to precise, data-driven digital strategies. As tools like CRM systems, marketing automation, and AI-powered analytics continue to advance, businesses have more opportunities to optimize engagement, improve efficiency, and refine their messaging.

However, as MarTech becomes more sophisticated, companies must also navigate challenges such as system integration, data privacy, and the complexity of managing multiple platforms. A strategic approach to adopting and leveraging these technologies—while maintaining a human-centric focus—will be key to long-term success.

Looking ahead, innovations in AI, blockchain, and immersive experiences like AR and VR will further shape the marketing landscape. Businesses that stay agile, embrace emerging trends, and prioritize ethical data usage will be best positioned to adapt to the continuously evolving digital ecosystem.

Key Takeaways

- Marketing has transitioned to a digital-first approach driven by technological advancements.
- MarTech tools, including CRM systems, marketing automation platforms, and data analytics, have streamlined marketing processes, making them more efficient and data driven.
- AI has further enhanced marketing by improving personalization, predictive analytics, and automated campaign management.
- While MarTech offers many advantages, businesses must address challenges such as data privacy, integration complexity, and the cost of implementation.

Reflection Questions

- Which MarTech tools do you currently use, and how have they improved your marketing processes?
- What challenges have you encountered when integrating new marketing technologies, and how have you addressed them?
- How can AI-driven personalization be applied to enhance customer engagement in your business?
- What emerging marketing technologies do you find most relevant to your future strategy?

Action Steps

- Assess your current marketing approach and identify any areas where technology could improve efficiency or targeting.
- Research and compare different marketing automation tools to find one that aligns with your business needs.
- Evaluate your data collection and management practices to ensure compliance with data privacy regulations.
- Experience AI-driven tools, such as chatbots or predictive analytics, to gain insights into customer behavior and improve marketing performance.
- Develop a phased plan for integrating new MarTech solutions while ensuring seamless alignment with existing systems.

MODULE 3
UNDERSTANDING AI AND ITS ROLE IN MARKETING

Artificial Intelligence (AI) has become a transformative force in marketing, enabling businesses to leverage advanced technologies such as machine learning, natural language processing, and predictive analytics. By utilizing AI, marketers can analyze vast datasets, uncover patterns, and automate repetitive tasks, leading to improved efficiency, customer engagement, and campaign performance. As AI continues to evolve, its integration into marketing strategies is reshaping the way businesses interact with their audiences, making data-driven decision-making more accessible and impactful.

The adoption of AI in marketing is driven by the need to process large amounts of customer data and extract actionable insights. Traditional marketing methods, which often rely on intuition and manual analysis, are increasingly being supplemented or replaced by AI-driven approaches. This shift allows marketers to better understand consumer behavior, personalize interactions, and optimize marketing strategies in real-time. The role of AI is not to replace human marketers but to enhance their capabilities by providing deeper insights and streamlining processes.

THE CORE COMPONENTS OF AI IN MARKETING

AI in marketing is built upon several key components that work together to improve various aspects of digital marketing campaigns.

These components include:

Machine Learning (ML)

Machine learning is a subset of AI that enables algorithms to learn from historical data and continuously refine their predictions and decision-making processes. In marketing, ML is extensively used for customer segmentation, lead scoring, and predictive analytics. Through analyzing past consumer behaviors and interactions, ML models detect trends and suggest optimal marketing strategies. For example, e-commerce platforms use ML to analyze purchasing patterns and recommend relevant products, while advertisers apply ML to optimize ad targeting and improve engagement rates. The iterative learning capability of ML ensures that as more data becomes available, predictions and decisions become increasingly refined, making marketing efforts more precise and efficient.

Natural Language Processing (NLP)

Natural Language Processing enables AI to understand, interpret, and generate human-like text, allowing businesses to automate customer interactions and create personalized content. NLP powers chatbots, virtual assistants, and sentiment analysis tools, which improve communication between brands and customers. AI-driven chatbots assist with customer queries, enhancing response times and reducing reliance on human agents. Sentiment analysis enables brands to gauge customer opinions by analyzing online reviews and social media conversations, informing their engagement strategies. Additionally, NLP facilitates content optimization by helping marketers tailor their messaging to different audiences, ensuring a consistent and relevant tone across various communication channels.

Computer Vision

Computer vision enables AI to interpret and analyze visual content such as images and videos, making it an invaluable tool for visual-based marketing strategies. Social media platforms, retail brands, and advertisers use AI-driven image recognition to tag products, suggest related items, and enhance user experiences. For instance, platforms like Pinterest and Google Lens utilize computer vision to enable visual search, allowing users to find similar products by uploading an image. Brands also apply AI-powered image analysis to track user-generated content, monitor brand sentiment, and detect fraudulent or inappropriate visual content. As visual content continues to dominate digital spaces, computer vision will play a crucial role in improving audience engagement and marketing precision.

Predictive Analytics

Predictive analytics leverages AI to analyze historical and real-time data, forecasting future trends in consumer behavior, campaign performance, and market dynamics. Businesses use predictive analytics to anticipate customer needs, adjust pricing strategies, and optimize marketing expenses. For example, retailers analyze seasonal purchasing trends to stock the right inventory, while digital marketers assess past engagement metrics to fine-tune upcoming campaigns. AI-powered predictive modeling helps identify high-value leads, increasing conversion rates by allowing marketers to focus on prospects most likely to make a purchase. The combination of historical and real-time insights equips businesses with the foresight to make informed marketing decisions, ultimately improving customer retention and revenue growth.

Automation

AI-driven automation enhances efficiency in marketing by handling repetitive tasks such as content generation, customer segmentation, and lead nurturing. By automating processes like email marketing, social media posting, and customer outreach, businesses can maintain consistency while reducing manual effort. For example, AI-driven email platforms analyze recipient behaviors to determine the optimal time to send emails, increasing open rates and engagement. Automated content personalization ensures that users receive recommendations based on their preferences, improving the overall customer experience. Moreover, AI-powered automation streamlines ad bidding in programmatic advertising, ensuring real-time adjustments for maximum effectiveness. As businesses seek to scale their marketing efforts, AI-driven automation will continue to be an essential component of modern marketing strategies.

AI APPLICATIONS IN MARKETING

AI is applied across multiple areas of marketing, revolutionizing how brands interact with their customers and optimize their strategies.

Customer Insights and Data Analysis

AI enhances marketers' ability to analyze large datasets from multiple sources, such as social media, website interactions, and purchasing behavior. AI-driven analytics identify trends, preferences, and behavioral patterns, allowing for precise targeting and segmentation. This results in more relevant marketing messages that reach the right audience at the right time. Businesses leverage AI to track evolving customer behaviors, refine their campaigns, and improve engagement rates by making data-driven decisions. Additionally, AI can help marketers predict shifts in consumer demand and industry trends, enabling proactive strategy adjustments.

Personalization and Customer Experience

AI-driven personalization analyzes various data points, including browsing history, purchase habits, and engagement metrics, to tailor recommendations and marketing content for individual users. By implementing AI-powered recommendation engines, businesses can provide product suggestions that align with customer interests, thereby improving satisfaction and retention rates. Personalization also extends to email marketing, social media content, and website experiences, ensuring that users interact with content that is relevant to their needs. Effective personalization fosters stronger relationships between brands and consumers, leading to increased customer loyalty and higher conversion rates.

Content Generation and Optimization

AI tools assist marketers in generating high-quality content, including blog posts, product descriptions, and advertisements. These tools analyze audience preferences and engagement data to craft compelling messaging. AI-driven content generation platforms can suggest optimal wording, structure, and tone to maximize engagement. Furthermore, AI tools optimize content distribution by analyzing which formats and platforms yield the best results. Marketers can leverage AI insights to refine messaging strategies, improve audience engagement, and drive traffic through well-structured content marketing approaches.

Chatbots and Conversational AI

AI-powered chatbots and virtual assistants provide real-time customer interactions, answering queries, guiding users, and facilitating transactions. These AI tools improve customer service availability, ensuring that users receive prompt responses without requiring human intervention. Businesses implement conversational AI to enhance customer experience by offering 24/7 support, resolving inquiries efficiently, and improving overall satisfaction. Additionally, AI-driven chatbots collect and analyze customer feedback, enabling businesses to refine their services based on real-time input from consumers.

Programmatic Advertising

AI automates digital advertising by analyzing user data and optimizing ad placements in real time. Through AI-driven programmatic advertising, businesses can ensure that their ads reach relevant audiences with higher precision. AI continually adjusts ad targeting strategies based on user interactions, maximizing return on investment (ROI) while reducing wasted ad spend. These technologies allow for more efficient budget allocation, delivering personalized ads based on behavioral patterns and demographic insights.

Email Marketing Optimization

AI enhances email marketing strategies by automating segmentation, subject line testing, and send-time optimization. AI tools analyze subscriber interactions to personalize email content, ensuring higher open and conversion rates. AI-driven segmentation allows marketers to group audiences based on behavioral traits, increasing message relevance and engagement. Additionally, AI monitors email campaign performance, providing actionable insights that enable continuous refinement of marketing strategies.

BENEFITS OF AI IN MARKETING

Enhanced Efficiency

AI automates time-consuming tasks such as data analysis, content creation, and customer segmentation. By handling repetitive processes, AI allows marketers to dedicate more time to strategic planning and creative execution. This improves productivity and ensures that marketing teams can focus on developing high-impact campaigns rather than being bogged down by routine tasks. Additionally, automation reduces human errors and enhances the speed of executing marketing strategies.

Improved Decision-Making

AI-powered analytics process large amounts of data to provide actionable insights. These insights help marketers refine their campaigns by identifying what strategies work best and what needs improvement. AI-driven decision-making minimizes guesswork and provides evidence-based recommendations, leading to more effective marketing initiatives. Marketers can track key performance indicators, measure engagement levels, and predict trends with greater accuracy, ensuring that their decisions align with customer expectations and business objectives.

Greater Personalization

AI personalizes marketing messages by analyzing user behavior, past interactions, and preferences. AI-driven recommendation engines suggest products, services, and content tailored to each user's interests, enhancing the overall customer experience. Personalized marketing fosters a stronger connection between brands and consumers, increasing engagement and conversion rates. AI ensures that messages are delivered at the right time through the right channels, making marketing efforts more relevant and impactful.

Optimized Customer Engagement

AI-driven chatbots and recommendation engines ensure that customer interactions are timely and relevant. Chatbots provide instant responses to queries, improving customer support and reducing wait times. AI-powered recommendation systems analyze user activity to suggest products or services that align with their interests. These AI applications enhance customer engagement by making interactions seamless and responsive, leading to better customer satisfaction and loyalty.

Scalability

AI systems can process vast amounts of data and manage large-scale interactions, making marketing efforts more scalable. Businesses can use AI to handle customer inquiries, analyze massive datasets, and execute personalized campaigns efficiently, even as their audience grows. AI's ability to work with large volumes of data ensures consistency in marketing strategies, allowing companies to expand their reach without compromising on quality or efficiency.

CHALLENGES AND CONSIDERATIONS

Despite its benefits, AI in marketing presents several challenges, each requiring careful consideration and strategic planning to ensure successful integration and ethical application.

Data Privacy and Security

Companies must ensure ethical data collection practices, transparency in how consumer data is used, and adherence to legal guidelines. Failure to do so can result in loss of consumer trust and potential legal penalties. Businesses should implement robust cybersecurity measures to protect sensitive data from breaches and unauthorized access. Additionally, providing consumers with control over their data—such as clear opt-in and opt-out mechanisms—can enhance brand credibility and foster stronger customer relationships.

Implementation Complexity

The integration of AI into existing marketing infrastructures is often complex and resource intensive. AI tools and platforms require substantial financial investment, technological expertise, and ongoing maintenance to function effectively. Businesses must train their teams to use AI-driven insights and automation effectively. A phased approach, starting with simpler AI applications—such as chatbots or predictive analytics—can help ease the transition. Moreover, seamless integration with existing marketing technology stacks ensures that AI solutions complement, rather than disrupt, current workflows. Companies should assess their technological readiness and create a structured roadmap for AI adoption to maximize efficiency and minimize operational disruptions.

Dependence on Quality Data

AI models rely on vast quantities of high-quality, accurate data to produce reliable and actionable insights. However, incomplete, outdated, or biased data can lead to flawed predictions and ineffective marketing strategies. To mitigate this risk, businesses should invest in robust data management practices, including regular data cleaning, validation, and updating. Implementing a data governance framework that ensures consistency, accuracy, and ethical data usage is critical. Additionally, businesses should source data from diverse and representative datasets to avoid algorithmic biases that may result in misleading marketing insights or unintended discrimination in target audiences.

Human Oversight and Bias

While AI can streamline marketing processes and improve efficiency, human oversight is crucial to ensure ethical decision-making and to mitigate biases within AI algorithms. AI models are only as unbiased as the data they are trained on, and without proper supervision, these biases can result in skewed recommendations, exclusion of certain demographics, or reinforcement of stereotypes. Businesses should regularly audit their AI systems to identify and rectify biases and maintain fairness in marketing campaigns. Additionally, the combination of AI-driven insights with human intuition and expertise can lead to more balanced and ethical decision-making. Establishing clear ethical guidelines for AI usage in marketing and involving cross-disciplinary teams in AI governance can further enhance responsible implementation.

THE FUTURE OF AI IN MARKETING

AI's role in marketing will continue to expand, introducing new innovations and trends:

AI-Powered Voice and Visual Search

Voice search and visual search are becoming more prevalent due to advancements in AI-driven natural language processing and image recognition. Consumers are increasingly using voice-activated assistants and image search tools to find information, shop for products, and interact with brands. This shift in search behavior requires marketers to optimize their content for voice queries by focusing on conversational keywords and structuring information to align with spoken language patterns. Similarly, brands must ensure that their visual content is easily recognizable by AI-powered search engines by using high-quality images, relevant metadata, and structured image descriptions. The evolution of voice and visual search presents new opportunities for businesses to enhance user experiences and improve search visibility.

Hyper-Personalization

AI-driven personalization is moving beyond traditional segmentation methods to deliver more precise and contextually relevant marketing experiences. Hyper-personalization utilizes real-time data, behavioral insights, and machine learning algorithms to tailor content, product recommendations, and promotional offers to individual users. Unlike conventional personalization techniques that rely on demographic and past behavior data, hyper-personalization adapts dynamically to changes in user preferences and interactions. By leveraging AI, brands can create adaptive marketing campaigns that respond to customer needs instantaneously, fostering deeper engagement and increasing customer retention rates. However, businesses must strike a balance between personalization and data privacy to maintain consumer trust and comply with regulatory requirements.

AI-Generated Content

Content creation is transforming with the integration of AI-driven tools that assist in generating written, visual, and video-based content. AI can analyze audience preferences, identify trending topics, and produce relevant content efficiently. While AI-generated content can streamline production workflows, human oversight remains crucial to ensure creativity, originality, and brand alignment. Marketers can leverage AI to enhance content ideation, improve engagement metrics, and automate repetitive tasks, such as drafting social media posts and generating product descriptions. As AI content-generation tools continue to improve, they will play a greater role in supporting content strategies without replacing the need for human creativity and storytelling.

Ethical AI Practices

With the increasing reliance on AI in marketing, ethical considerations are becoming more significant. Issues such as data privacy, algorithmic bias, and transparency in AI decision-making are critical concerns for businesses and consumers alike. Brands that prioritize ethical AI practices must establish clear guidelines for data usage, ensure fairness in AI-driven decision-making, and maintain transparency about how AI influences marketing strategies. Implementing AI ethically involves regular audits of AI models, addressing biases in data, and providing consumers with control over their data preferences. By adopting responsible AI practices, businesses can build consumer trust and establish long-term credibility in the digital marketplace.

AI is increasingly shaping the way businesses approach marketing, offering tools that enhance efficiency, personalization, and data-driven decision-making. By integrating AI-powered technologies such as machine learning, natural language processing, and predictive analytics, marketers can optimize their strategies, automate repetitive tasks, and better understand customer behavior.

While AI presents clear advantages, its successful implementation requires addressing challenges such as data privacy, integration complexity, and the need for human oversight. Ethical considerations, including fairness in AI decision-making and responsible data usage, will remain key factors in ensuring that AI-driven marketing practices build consumer trust rather than erode it.

Looking ahead, advancements in AI-powered search, hyper-personalization, and content generation will continue to refine how businesses engage with their audiences. Organizations that adopt AI strategically—balancing automation with human expertise—will be well-positioned to adapt to evolving consumer expectations and create more meaningful, data-informed marketing experiences.

Key Takeaways

- AI plays an important role in marketing by analyzing data, predicting consumer behavior, and automating repetitive tasks.
- Key AI technologies include machine learning, natural language processing, predictive analytics, and automation, each contributing to marketing efficiency and precision.
- AI-driven applications such as chatbots, personalization engines, and programmatic advertising enhance customer engagement and optimize marketing performance.
- AI improves efficiency by automating content generation, campaign management, and audience segmentation while enabling better decision-making through data-driven insights.
- Challenges such as data privacy, implementation, and algorithmic biases must be addressed to ensure effective AI adoption in marketing.

Reflection Questions

- How do you see AI transforming your current marketing strategies?
- Which AI-driven marketing tools have you used, and how effective have they been?
- What are some challenges you anticipate when implementing AI in your marketing processes?
- How can AI help you improve customer experience and engagement in your business?
- What ethical considerations should businesses keep in mind when using AI in marketing?

Action Steps

- Identify an area in your marketing strategy that could benefit from AI-driven automation or analytics.
- Research AI-powered tools that align with your business needs, such as chatbots, predictive analytics, or content optimization platforms.
- Experiment with a small-scale AI-driven initiative, such as an AI-powered recommendation engine or automated customer segmentation, to test its effectiveness.
- Develop a plan for integrating AI into your marketing efforts, balancing automation with human oversight.

PART II
AI-DRIVEN STRATEGIES AND DATA-DRIVEN INSIGHTS

MODULE 4
INTEGRATING AI WITH MARKETING TECHNOLOGY PLATFORMS

The integration of Artificial Intelligence (AI) with Marketing Technology (MarTech) platforms has reshaped how businesses develop, execute, and refine their marketing strategies. AI enhances marketing tools by automating processes, generating data-driven insights, and facilitating personalized customer engagement. As a result, businesses can make more informed decisions, improve customer interactions, and streamline their workflows.

This chapter explores the significance of AI in MarTech integration, examining key areas where AI is making an impact, the challenges businesses may encounter, and best practices for successful implementation. By understanding these aspects, businesses can leverage AI to enhance their marketing efforts, optimize operations, and achieve measurable outcomes.

UNDERSTANDING AI INTEGRATION IN MARTECH

MarTech consists of various tools used by businesses to manage and optimize their marketing activities. These tools include customer relationship management (CRM) systems, email marketing platforms, content management systems (CMS), social media management tools, and data analytics platforms. AI integration enhances these systems by automating processes, analyzing large datasets, and providing actionable insights. Some key AI-driven capabilities in MarTech include:

Predictive Analytics

AI-powered predictive analytics allows businesses to forecast trends, customer behavior, and campaign performance by analyzing historical data. This involves examining past customer interactions, purchase patterns, and engagement metrics to identify trends that can inform future marketing strategies. For example, businesses can use predictive analytics to determine which products are likely to experience increased demand during specific seasons or identify customer segments more likely to respond to a particular promotion.

By leveraging predictive analytics, companies can optimize inventory management, create more targeted marketing campaigns, and improve customer retention efforts. Furthermore, AI-powered models continuously refine their predictions by learning from new data, ensuring that insights remain relevant and accurate. However, organizations must ensure they have access to high-quality data to maximize the effectiveness of predictive analytics.

Customer Segmentation

AI facilitates dynamic customer segmentation by analyzing vast datasets and identifying patterns within customer demographics, behaviors, and engagement levels. Traditional segmentation methods often rely on broad demographic factors, but AI enhances this process by incorporating real-time behavioral insights, such as browsing habits, purchase history, and interaction frequency.

By using AI-driven segmentation, businesses can create highly tailored marketing strategies that address the specific needs of different customer groups. For instance, an AI system can identify customers who frequently purchase high-end products and segment them for premium offers, while another segment may consist of first-time buyers who require more educational content before making a purchase decision.

Additionally, AI-driven customer segmentation allows businesses to personalize their communication strategies, ensuring that messages resonate with each audience group. This improves customer satisfaction and increases the likelihood of conversions. Companies should ensure they collect and analyze relevant data to achieve meaningful segmentation insights.

Personalized Content Recommendations

AI enables businesses to deliver personalized content recommendations by analyzing individual user behavior, preferences, and engagement history. This is commonly seen in e-commerce platforms, streaming services, and content-based websites, where AI suggests products, movies, or articles based on previous interactions.

For example, an AI-driven recommendation engine can analyze a user's past purchases and browsing history to suggest complementary products. Similarly, streaming platforms use AI to curate personalized playlists or suggest new content based on a viewer's watching habits. The effectiveness of personalized recommendations relies on real-time data processing, allowing businesses to adjust their strategies based on evolving user preferences.

By implementing AI-driven personalization, businesses can enhance customer experience, encourage repeat engagement, and drive higher conversion rates. However, companies must also be mindful of privacy concerns and ensure that they use customer data ethically and transparently.

Marketing Automation

AI enhances marketing automation by optimizing email campaigns, social media scheduling, and ad targeting to increase efficiency.

Traditional marketing automation relies on predefined workflows, whereas AI-driven automation continuously refines these workflows based on real-time data insights.

For instance, AI can determine the best times to send emails to specific customer segments, increasing the likelihood of engagement. It can also optimize social media posts by analyzing historical performance data to schedule posts when engagement rates are highest. Additionally, AI-driven automation helps businesses manage ad campaigns more effectively by adjusting bidding strategies and targeting based on user behavior.

AI-powered automation reduces the manual effort required in executing marketing campaigns, allowing businesses to focus on strategy and creativity. While automation improves efficiency, businesses should also monitor AI-driven processes to ensure they align with their brand's overall marketing objectives.

Chatbots and Conversational AI

AI-powered chatbots enhance customer support by offering real-time responses and assistance. These chatbots use natural language processing (NLP) to understand and respond to customer queries in a conversational manner.

Businesses implement chatbots to handle routine inquiries, such as order status updates, product recommendations, and troubleshooting guidance. By automating these interactions, companies can provide immediate support to customers while reducing the workload on human agents. More advanced chatbots integrate machine learning to improve their responses over time, offering more accurate and context-aware assistance.

Conversational AI is also used in virtual assistants and voice search technology, providing a seamless way for customers to interact with businesses. However, organizations should ensure that chatbot interactions feel natural and human-like to maintain customer satisfaction. While AI-driven chatbots enhance efficiency, having human support available for complex issues remains essential.

By integrating AI into MarTech tools, businesses can refine their marketing campaigns, enhance customer relationships, and make data-driven decisions that drive growth.

KEY AREAS OF AI INTEGRATION IN MARTECH

Customer Relationship Management (CRM) Systems

CRM systems play a crucial role in managing customer interactions, tracking sales activities, and maintaining valuable customer data. AI integration in CRM platforms improves their efficiency and effectiveness by automating various processes that traditionally require manual effort.

AI-driven CRMs can streamline operations by automating data entry, reducing manual errors, and improving data accuracy. By utilizing machine learning algorithms, AI identifies patterns in historical customer interactions, allowing businesses to personalize communication and predict customer needs. Predictive modeling helps organizations anticipate customer behavior and provide relevant recommendations, improving engagement and retention.

AI also enhances lead scoring by analyzing various factors, such as customer interactions, purchase history, and engagement levels, to identify high-value prospects. This allows sales teams to prioritize their efforts on leads that have a higher likelihood of conversion. AI-powered recommendation engines can further guide sales representatives with tailored suggestions for follow-ups and engagement strategies based on real-time insights.

Beyond customer engagement, AI in CRM systems supports workflow automation by scheduling follow-up emails, sending reminders, and generating customer reports. These automation capabilities free up sales and marketing teams to focus on strategic decision-making rather than administrative tasks.

Additionally, AI-driven sentiment analysis can help businesses gauge customer satisfaction by analyzing feedback, reviews, and customer support interactions. By understanding customer sentiment, organizations can proactively address concerns and enhance the overall customer experience. As AI continues to evolve, CRM platforms will become more intuitive, providing real-time insights that enable businesses to build stronger relationships with their customers.

Email Marketing and AI-Powered Campaigns

AI-driven email marketing tools optimize engagement and conversion rates by leveraging automation and data analytics to deliver relevant content to users. These tools dynamically segment audiences based on behavior, interests, and past interactions, ensuring that marketing messages resonate with the right recipients.

AI-powered email platforms use natural language processing (NLP) and machine learning to optimize subject lines, email content, and call-to-action placements, improving open and click-through rates. By analyzing historical email performance, AI algorithms can suggest improvements that align with audience preferences.

Email marketing automation benefits from AI by determining the best times to send messages based on user activity and engagement patterns. Instead of sending mass emails at a fixed schedule, AI personalizes delivery times to align with when each recipient is most likely to engage. This increases the likelihood of customer interactions and conversions.

Furthermore, AI-driven email marketing platforms provide deep insights into campaign performance by tracking user interactions, engagement levels, and conversion rates. Marketers can use these insights to refine strategies, test different content variations, and improve targeting audiences.

By utilizing AI-powered email marketing, businesses can increase customer retention through personalized content, automated follow-ups, and targeted messaging strategies that enhance the overall effectiveness of email campaigns.

Content Management Systems (CMS) and AI-Driven Content Optimization

AI enhances content creation, distribution, and performance analysis in CMS platforms by leveraging data analytics to improve content relevance and reach. AI-driven CMS solutions assist marketers in generating ideas for blog posts, articles, and website content by analyzing trending topics and audience interests.

Automating metadata tagging is another key AI capability that improves search engine optimization (SEO). AI-driven CMS platforms analyze content and assign appropriate metadata, ensuring that web pages rank higher in search engine results. Additionally, AI tools optimize content by assessing readability, tone, and engagement levels, providing suggestions for improvement.

AI enhances user engagement by recommending personalized content based on browsing behavior. By analyzing user interactions, AI dynamically suggests relevant articles, videos, or product pages that align with individual preferences. This keeps users engaged for longer periods, increasing the likelihood of conversions.

Performance analytics play a crucial role in content marketing strategies, and AI-driven insights provide valuable data on which types of content perform best. AI can track engagement metrics such as page views, bounce rates, and time spent on each page, allowing businesses to refine their content strategies based on real-time feedback.

By leveraging AI in CMS platforms, businesses can enhance content discoverability, engagement, and personalization, leading to more impactful marketing efforts.

Social Media Management and AI Automation

AI-powered social media tools help businesses manage and optimize their online presence by automating content scheduling, analyzing engagement metrics, and identifying trends. AI streamlines social media management by automatically scheduling posts based on audience activity, ensuring maximum visibility and interaction.

AI-driven analytics assess user engagement patterns and provide insights into the most effective content types, posting times, and audience preferences. By analyzing sentiment in user comments and interactions, businesses can gauge public perception and adjust their strategies accordingly.

AI-powered tools also assist in identifying key influencers and brand advocates by analyzing engagement levels and network reach. Businesses can leverage these insights to develop partnerships with influencers who align with their brand values and marketing objectives.

By integrating AI into social media management, businesses can maintain a consistent posting schedule, track audience sentiment, and refine engagement strategies based on real-time data.

AI in Paid Advertising and Programmatic Marketing

AI-driven advertising platforms enhance the effectiveness of paid marketing efforts by optimizing ad placements, targeting the right audience segments, and reducing ad fraud. AI automates bid adjustments in real-time, ensuring that businesses maximize their advertising budgets.

By analyzing performance data, AI identifies high-performing ad creatives and refines marketing messages to improve engagement. AI also enables precise audience targeting by leveraging behavioral data to serve relevant ads to users most likely to convert.

AI-powered fraud detection mechanisms help reduce ad fraud by identifying suspicious activities, such as bot-driven clicks and fake impressions. By minimizing fraudulent activities, businesses can ensure that their ad spend is used efficiently.

By incorporating AI into paid advertising, businesses can improve ROI, optimize targeting, and enhance overall ad performance through data-driven decision-making.

BENEFITS OF AI INTEGRATION IN MARTECH

Increased Efficiency

AI plays a crucial role in automating repetitive tasks, allowing businesses to focus on more strategic initiatives. By minimizing the need for manual intervention, AI enhances operational efficiency across various marketing functions. For instance, AI-powered tools can automate customer data entry, content scheduling, and lead qualification processes, reducing the time employees spend on administrative tasks. Additionally, AI-driven workflow automation streamlines cross-functional collaboration, ensuring that marketing campaigns are executed in a timely and coordinated manner. However, businesses must balance automation with human oversight to maintain quality and relevance in their marketing efforts.

Enhanced Personalization

AI enables businesses to create personalized experiences by analyzing customer data and predicting individual preferences. By leveraging machine learning models, marketers can tailor content, product recommendations, and promotional offers based on a customer's past interactions. AI-powered personalization extends beyond email marketing and into website experiences, where dynamic content adapts in real-time based on user behavior.

Chatbots and virtual assistants also contribute to enhanced personalization by providing immediate and context-aware responses to customer inquiries. While AI-driven personalization enhances engagement, businesses should ensure ethical data practices and transparency to build trust with their customers.

Improved Decision-Making

AI analytics provide valuable insights that help businesses refine their marketing strategies. By processing large volumes of data, AI can identify patterns and trends that may not be immediately apparent through traditional analysis. For example, AI can assess the effectiveness of past marketing campaigns and recommend adjustments for future initiatives. AI-driven dashboards and reporting tools provide marketers with actionable insights, enabling data-driven decision-making. However, while AI enhances decision-making capabilities, it is important to combine AI-generated insights with human expertise to account for contextual nuances and external market dynamics.

Better Customer Engagement

AI fosters real-time customer interactions, improving engagement and responsiveness. AI-powered chatbots, voice assistants, and sentiment analysis tools enable businesses to interact with customers across multiple channels seamlessly. These tools ensure that customer queries are addressed promptly, enhancing the overall user experience. AI-driven engagement also extends to social media monitoring, where businesses can assess audience sentiment and adjust their messaging accordingly. While AI enhances customer engagement, companies should maintain a human touch in their interactions to build meaningful relationships with their audience.

Optimized Marketing Spend

AI helps businesses allocate resources effectively by leveraging predictive analytics. By analyzing customer behavior, market trends, and campaign performance, AI can optimize budget distribution across different marketing channels. For example, AI-powered ad platforms adjust bidding strategies in real-time, ensuring cost-effective advertising placements. Additionally, AI can identify underperforming campaigns and suggest reallocations to higher-performing channels. By improving budget efficiency, AI enables businesses to achieve better returns on their marketing investments. However, businesses should continuously monitor AI-driven budget allocations to ensure alignment with broader marketing objectives.

CHALLENGES OF AI INTEGRATION IN MARKETING TECHNOLOGY

Data Privacy and Compliance

As businesses integrate AI-driven tools into their marketing strategies, they must navigate an evolving landscape of data privacy and compliance regulations. Laws such as GDPR set strict guidelines on how businesses can collect, store, and use customer data. AI-powered marketing tools rely heavily on data to function effectively, but businesses must ensure that their data-handling practices align with these legal requirements.

To maintain compliance, companies should implement clear policies regarding data collection, ensure transparency with consumers about how their information is used, and secure explicit consent where required. This includes updating privacy policies, offering opt-out mechanisms, and ensuring that AI models only process necessary data. Additionally, organizations should invest in secure data storage solutions, encryption, and regular audits to detect and mitigate potential security vulnerabilities.

Failing to adhere to data privacy laws can result in legal consequences, including fines and reputational damage. Therefore, businesses should establish compliance frameworks, work closely with legal teams, and train employees on data protection best practices. AI-driven marketing strategies should balance personalization with privacy protection to build customer trust while maintaining legal compliance.

System Compatibility and Integration Complexity

Integrating AI solutions into existing MarTech stacks can be a complex process, requiring technical expertise and careful planning. Many businesses use multiple marketing platforms, such as Customer Relationship Management (CRM) systems, email marketing tools, analytics dashboards, and social media management tools. Ensuring AI-powered tools can seamlessly interact with these existing systems is crucial for maximizing their effectiveness.

One of the main challenges of AI integration is the need for robust APIs (Application Programming Interfaces) and middleware that enable different systems to communicate. Businesses may face issues such as incompatibility between legacy systems and newer AI-driven solutions, leading to additional costs for upgrades or custom development.

To minimize integration challenges, organizations should conduct a thorough assessment of their existing MarTech infrastructure before adopting AI solutions. Selecting AI tools that offer native integrations with widely used platforms can streamline the process. Additionally, IT teams should collaborate closely with marketing departments to ensure smooth implementation, data synchronization, and workflow continuity.

Ongoing system maintenance and updates are also necessary to keep AI solutions functioning optimally. Businesses should allocate resources for regular monitoring, troubleshooting, and training employees on using AI-enhanced tools effectively.

Data Quality and Availability

AI models require high-quality data to generate accurate and meaningful insights. If the data used to train AI models is incomplete, outdated, or biased, the resulting predictions and recommendations may be unreliable. Poor data quality can lead to ineffective marketing campaigns, misguided customer targeting, and inaccurate performance analysis.

Businesses must establish strong data governance policies to ensure that their datasets are clean, relevant, and well-structured. This includes implementing automated data cleansing processes to remove duplicate or erroneous information, standardizing data formats, and ensuring real-time data updates. Organizations should also define clear data collection methods, ensuring that inputs from different marketing channels are accurate and consistent.

AI-driven tools should be continuously monitored to identify any discrepancies in the data they process. Additionally, businesses should use data augmentation techniques to enhance existing datasets and improve AI model accuracy. Collaborating with data scientists and analytics professionals can help marketers interpret AI-generated insights more effectively and refine data strategies for improved outcomes.

Cost of AI Implementation

Adopting AI in marketing technology requires investment in software, infrastructure, and employee training. AI-powered solutions can range from off-the-shelf tools to custom-built models tailored to a business's specific needs. Companies must evaluate the costs associated with AI adoption and determine whether the expected return on investment (ROI) justifies the expenditure. Key cost considerations include:

Software Licensing | AI-driven marketing platforms often require subscription fees or licensing agreements, which can vary based on features and usage limits.

Infrastructure and Cloud Computing | AI solutions that process large amounts of data may require cloud-based computing power, which adds to operational costs.

Training and Upskilling | Employees must be trained to effectively use AI-driven tools, interpret insights, and integrate them into marketing strategies.

Maintenance and Support | Regular software updates, troubleshooting, and AI model retraining require ongoing investment.

To optimize costs, businesses should start with pilot projects that test AI applications on a small scale before committing to full implementation. Additionally, leveraging pre-built AI tools with flexible pricing models can be a cost-effective alternative to developing custom solutions. Evaluating long-term benefits, such as efficiency gains, improved targeting, and increased revenue, can help businesses make informed investment decisions.

Human Oversight and Ethical Concerns

While AI enhances marketing efficiency, it is important to maintain human oversight to ensure ethical and responsible usage. AI models can sometimes reflect biases present in the training data, leading to unintended discrimination in customer targeting, content recommendations, or automated decision-making processes.

For instance, if an AI-driven ad platform unintentionally favors certain demographics while excluding others, it could result in biased marketing strategies that negatively impact inclusivity and brand reputation. Businesses must actively address these concerns by auditing AI models for bias, ensuring diversity in training datasets, and implementing guidelines for ethical AI usage.

Transparency is another key factor in the adoption of ethical AI. Companies should clearly communicate how AI is used in their marketing efforts and provide customers with options to control their data and preferences. AI-generated content, such as chatbots and automated emails, should be distinguishable from human interactions to avoid misleading customers.

Additionally, businesses should establish an AI governance framework, where dedicated teams oversee AI-driven marketing strategies and ensure compliance with ethical standards. While AI can optimize marketing operations, human input remains essential in interpreting AI-generated insights, making strategic decisions, and fostering meaningful customer relationships.

BEST PRACTICES FOR AI INTEGRATION IN MARTECH

Assess Business Needs and Goals

Before integrating AI into marketing technology, businesses should conduct a comprehensive assessment of their needs and objectives. AI can enhance various aspects of marketing, such as customer segmentation, personalized content delivery, and performance analytics. Identifying the areas where AI can provide the most value ensures a focused implementation strategy. Businesses should start by evaluating existing pain points and determining how AI can help resolve them. Additionally, setting clear key performance indicators (KPIs) helps in tracking the effectiveness of AI integration. Without a well-defined strategy, companies may invest in AI tools that do not align with their marketing goals, leading to inefficient resource utilization.

Choose AI Tools That Align with Existing Infrastructure

Selecting AI-powered MarTech solutions that integrate seamlessly with current platforms ensures smoother adoption and usability.

Businesses often use various tools such as CRM systems, content management platforms, and email marketing software. AI tools should complement these existing systems to avoid workflow disruptions. Compatibility should be a primary consideration when evaluating AI solutions. Businesses should also consider whether cloud-based or on-premise AI tools suit their infrastructure needs. Proper integration reduces operational silos and allows AI-driven insights to be leveraged across different departments, enhancing collaboration and decision-making.

Ensure Data Quality and Governance

AI models rely on data to generate insights, and the accuracy of these insights depends on the quality of the data provided. Businesses should establish strong data governance practices to maintain data integrity. This includes ensuring that data is accurate, up-to-date, and structured in a way that AI systems can process efficiently. Organizations should also address data security concerns and compliance requirements, particularly when dealing with customer information. Implementing data validation processes and periodic audits can help businesses maintain high data standards, ultimately leading to more reliable AI-driven insights.

Adopt a Gradual Implementation Approach

Rather than overhauling existing systems, businesses should start with small AI-driven pilot projects and scale up based on performance. This approach minimizes risks and allows organizations to evaluate the effectiveness of AI before full deployment. A phased implementation enables marketing teams to familiarize themselves with AI tools gradually. Additionally, businesses can assess AI's impact on marketing efficiency and make necessary adjustments before expanding usage. Gathering feedback from employees and analyzing initial results help organizations refine their AI strategies for broader adoption.

Monitor AI Performance and Continuously Optimize

Once AI tools are integrated into MarTech platforms, businesses should regularly evaluate their performance. AI models require continuous monitoring to ensure they remain effective and aligned with marketing objectives. Performance metrics should be analyzed to determine whether AI-driven strategies are delivering expected outcomes. Additionally, businesses should update AI models with new data to improve their predictive capabilities. Periodic reviews allow companies to optimize AI applications, refine algorithms, and adjust marketing strategies based on data-driven insights. Continuous improvement ensures AI remains an asset in enhancing marketing efforts rather than becoming an underutilized tool.

Educating Teams on AI Adoption

Successful AI implementation depends on how well marketing teams understand and utilize AI-driven tools. Providing training sessions and educational resources helps employees adapt to AI-enhanced workflows. AI should not be seen as a replacement for human creativity and strategy but rather as a tool that enhances decision-making and efficiency. Encouraging cross-functional collaboration between AI specialists and marketing professionals fosters a better understanding of AI's capabilities. Businesses should also establish internal knowledge-sharing initiatives to keep teams informed about AI advancements and best practices, ensuring long-term success in AI integration.

THE FUTURE OF AI IN MARTECH INTEGRATION

AI is expected to play an increasingly significant role in MarTech. Some emerging trends include:

AI-Generated Content

AI-driven tools are becoming integral to content creation, providing businesses with the ability to generate text, images, and videos tailored to specific audiences. These tools analyze data from past engagements, user preferences, and industry trends to create content that aligns with audience interests. Businesses can leverage AI-generated content for blog posts, social media captions, email marketing campaigns, and even video scripts.

One of the key advantages of AI-generated content is efficiency. Marketers can use AI-powered tools to quickly draft multiple variations of content, experiment with different tones, and adjust messaging based on performance insights. This does not eliminate the need for human oversight; instead, it augments the creative process, allowing marketing teams to focus on strategy and refinement.

However, businesses must ensure that AI-generated content aligns with brand voice and maintains authenticity. Additionally, there is a growing discussion around ethical considerations, such as ensuring transparency in AI-generated copy and preventing misleading or generic outputs. By implementing AI responsibly, businesses can improve content marketing efforts while maintaining credibility.

Voice and Visual Search Optimization

As consumers increasingly adopt voice assistants and image search technologies, businesses must optimize their content for these evolving search behaviors. AI-powered voice search relies on natural language processing (NLP) to understand spoken queries, while visual search allows users to upload images and receive relevant search results.

To stay relevant in this landscape, businesses should focus on optimizing their digital content for conversational queries. Unlike traditional text-based search, voice search queries are typically longer and structured in a natural, question-based format. Optimizing website content with FAQs, structured data, and natural phrasing can improve search engine rankings for voice queries.

Similarly, visual search optimization involves ensuring that product images and metadata are properly labeled and tagged. AI-powered image recognition tools can analyze elements within images and match them with relevant search queries. Businesses in e-commerce, fashion, and home decor sectors, in particular, can benefit from optimizing their image-based content for visual search engines.

Hyper-Automation in Marketing Workflows

AI is driving the expansion of hyper-automation, where multiple marketing processes are automated to improve efficiency and consistency. Unlike traditional automation, which focuses on predefined workflows, hyper-automation involves the combination of AI, machine learning, and robotic process automation (RPA) to continuously analyze, optimize, and adjust marketing activities.

For example, hyper-automation can enhance lead generation by automatically qualifying leads based on real-time engagement metrics and demographic data. It can also optimize digital advertising by adjusting bids dynamically based on campaign performance, audience behavior, and external market conditions.

AI-powered chatbots and virtual assistants are another example of hyper-automation, enabling businesses to provide real-time customer support and personalized product recommendations. By integrating hyper-automation into marketing strategies, businesses can reduce manual effort, improve response times, and ensure seamless customer experience.

While hyper-automation increases efficiency, businesses should approach it strategically. Over-reliance on AI without human intervention may lead to impersonal interactions or missed contextual nuances in customer engagement. A balance between AI-driven automation and human decision-making is essential for effective implementation.

AI-Driven Predictive Customer Journeys

AI-driven predictive analytics allows businesses to map out customer journeys based on past behaviors and real-time data. By analyzing customer interactions across multiple touchpoints, AI models can predict which stage a user is in within the sales funnel and recommend personalized actions to guide them toward conversion.

For instance, predictive analytics can identify when a customer is likely to abandon a purchase and trigger an automated response, such as a personalized email reminder or a discount offer. Similarly, AI can analyze browsing patterns and recommend relevant content or products, enhancing the overall user experience.

Predictive customer journeys are particularly valuable for customer retention strategies. By understanding churn signals, businesses can proactively engage with at-risk customers through personalized offers or support initiatives. Additionally, AI-powered analytics can help businesses segment audiences based on their likelihood to convert, enabling more targeted marketing efforts.

Despite its advantages, predictive analytics requires high-quality data to generate accurate insights. Businesses must ensure that their data collection processes are robust and continuously updated to reflect changing customer behaviors. AI-driven predictive models should also be regularly reviewed and refined to ensure their effectiveness.

The integration of AI with marketing technology platforms is transforming how businesses manage customer interactions, optimize campaigns, and automate processes. By enhancing MarTech tools with AI-driven capabilities such as predictive analytics, automated customer segmentation, and personalized content recommendations, organizations can improve efficiency and deliver more relevant experiences to their audiences.

While AI-powered solutions offer significant advantages, their successful implementation requires addressing challenges such as data privacy, system integration, and maintaining data quality. Businesses must also ensure that AI-driven automation complements human oversight, allowing for strategic decision-making and ethical data usage.

As AI continues to evolve, emerging trends like hyper-automation, voice and visual search optimization, and predictive customer journeys will further shape marketing strategies. Companies that take a structured approach to AI adoption—aligning technology with business goals, ensuring seamless integration, and continuously optimizing their AI-driven tools—will be better positioned to navigate the changing digital landscape and create more effective, data-driven marketing experiences.

Key Takeaways

- AI integration with marketing technology (MarTech) platforms enhances automation, personalization, and data-driven decision-making.
- AI-driven predictive analytics improve forecasting, customer segmentation, and marketing strategy optimization.
- AI-powered chatbots and automation tools enhance customer interactions and streamline workflows.
- CRM systems, email marketing, content management, social media management, and programmatic advertising benefit from AI-driven enhancements.
- Challenges such as data privacy, system compatibility, and maintaining data quality must be addressed for successful AI adoption.

Reflection Questions

- How does your organization currently use AI in its marketing strategy?
- What MarTech tools do you rely on, and how could AI improve their effectiveness?
- What challenges do you anticipate in integrating AI into your marketing workflows?
- How can AI-driven automation help your marketing team optimize time and resources?
- What steps can you take to ensure ethical AI usage and compliance with data privacy regulations?

Action Steps

- Assess existing MarTech tools to identify opportunities for AI integration.
- Research AI-powered solutions that align with business objectives and customer engagement goals.
- Review current data collection practices to ensure AI-driven insights are based on accurate and high-quality data.
- Conduct a small-scale AI pilot project, such as implementing an AI-driven email segmentation tool or chatbot.
- Develop an AI governance framework to ensure ethical AI use and compliance with data regulations.

MODULE 5 DATA-DRIVEN DECISION MAKING WITH AI

Data has become more important than ever in modern marketing, helping businesses make smarter decisions and create more effective strategies. Data-driven decision-making (DDDM) has become an integral part of modern marketing, allowing businesses to analyze customer interactions, optimize campaigns, and refine marketing strategies based on real-time insights. The rise of Artificial Intelligence (AI) has significantly enhanced the efficiency of DDDM, enabling businesses to identify patterns, make accurate predictions, and automate data analysis processes at an unprecedented scale. AI-driven decision-making allows marketers to shift from traditional intuition-based strategies to more precise, data-backed approaches.

This chapter explores how AI facilitates data-driven decision-making, its critical applications in marketing analytics, the challenges businesses may encounter when implementing AI solutions, and the best practices to maximize the benefits of AI-driven insights. By understanding these aspects, businesses can make more informed and effective marketing decisions that align with customer expectations and market trends.

THE ROLE OF AI IN DATA-DRIVEN DECISION MAKING

AI plays a pivotal role in enhancing the efficiency and accuracy of marketing decisions. It enables businesses to process vast amounts of structured and unstructured data in real time, reducing human error and optimizing marketing efforts. AI-driven decision-making is transforming marketing in several ways:

Identifying Trends and Consumer Behavior Patterns

AI analyzes large sets of historical and real-time data from various sources, including website visits, social media interactions, and purchase histories, to uncover trends in customer behavior. Businesses can use these insights to refine their marketing strategies, personalize customer experiences, and predict emerging consumer preferences.

Improving Segmentation and Targeting

AI enables businesses to move beyond broad demographic segments by analyzing behavioral and psychographic data to create highly detailed customer profiles. These insights allow for the delivery of personalized marketing campaigns tailored to specific customer needs and interests, increasing engagement and conversion rates.

Predicting Campaign Performance

AI-driven models leverage historical marketing data and real-time customer interactions to predict how a campaign will perform before it is launched. By testing different variables, such as messaging, timing, and audience segments, businesses can refine their campaigns for maximum effectiveness and ROI.

Automating Reporting and Insights Generation

AI tools can process and visualize complex data sets, providing clear insights without requiring manual intervention. Automated reporting reduces the time required for analysis and allows marketing teams to focus on strategic decision-making rather than data processing.

Optimizing Marketing Spend

AI-driven analytics help businesses allocate budgets more effectively by analyzing the performance of various marketing channels in real-time. This enables marketers to shift spending towards the most effective strategies, reducing waste and improving overall marketing efficiency.

KEY AI-DRIVEN ANALYTICS IN MARKETING

Customer Behavior Analysis

Understanding customer behavior is crucial for optimizing marketing efforts. AI-powered analytics platforms collect and process data from multiple touchpoints, including website interactions, social media engagement, and purchase history. Businesses can gain insights into customer preferences, purchase intent, and engagement levels, allowing them to craft personalized marketing messages and product recommendations. By leveraging AI-driven behavior analysis, businesses can:

- Identify high-value customer segments.
- Understand browsing and purchasing trends.
- Enhance customer experience through tailored interactions.
- Optimize pricing strategies based on demand and customer behavior.

Predictive Analytics

Predictive analytics uses AI algorithms to forecast future customer behaviors and market trends. By analyzing past purchase data, browsing patterns, and engagement history, AI models predict:

- Potential churn risks and retention strategies.
- The likelihood of customers making repeat purchases.
- Seasonal or trend-based demand for specific products or services.

- The expected performance of marketing campaigns before launch.

Businesses that implement predictive analytics can make proactive adjustments to their strategies, ensuring better customer engagement and sales conversion rates.

Sentiment Analysis

AI-driven sentiment analysis scans customer feedback, product reviews, and social media conversations to gauge public perception of a brand. By assessing the sentiment behind customer interactions, businesses can:

- Identify common pain points and address them proactively.
- Adjust marketing messaging to align with customer sentiment.
- Track brand reputation in real time.
- Improve customer service responsiveness based on sentiment trends.

Marketing Attribution Analysis

Marketing attribution refers to identifying the impact of various marketing channels on customer conversions. AI helps businesses implement multi-touch attribution models, ensuring a more accurate understanding of which channels contribute the most to sales. This enables marketers to:

- Allocate budgets to high-performing channels.
- Optimize cross-channel marketing strategies.
- Enhance ad targeting based on channel effectiveness.

Real-Time Data Processing

AI processes real-time data from website visits, ad clicks, social media interactions, and email responses. This allows marketers to:

- Adjust ad targeting dynamically based on real-time engagement.

- Optimize email campaigns by identifying peak engagement times.
- Personalize customer experiences instantly based on browsing behavior.

BENEFITS OF AI-DRIVEN DECISION MAKING IN MARKETING

Improved Accuracy

AI reduces human bias in data analysis by relying on structured methodologies and pattern recognition. Traditional data analysis often involves human intuition, which can be influenced by subjective perspectives. AI minimizes errors by using objective data points, ensuring that insights are based on verifiable trends rather than assumptions. Businesses leveraging AI for accuracy can develop marketing campaigns that align more closely with consumer behavior and preferences. AI also enables organizations to refine their data models continuously, improving accuracy over time as more data is processed.

Faster Decision-Making

With the ability to process large volumes of data instantly, AI allows businesses to make informed decisions quickly. Traditional data analysis methods can be time-consuming, requiring manual data sorting and interpretation. AI-driven tools automate these processes, providing marketers with actionable insights in real time. The speed at which AI processes data allows organizations to respond to market trends, customer preferences, and competitive actions without delays. Faster decision-making leads to improved agility, enabling businesses to optimize their strategies more effectively.

Enhanced Customer Experience

AI-driven personalization enhances customer interactions by

analyzing user behavior, preferences, and past interactions. By using AI, businesses can deliver personalized recommendations, targeted advertisements, and tailored content that align with individual customer needs. This level of customization improves customer engagement by making interactions more relevant. AI also enables businesses to predict customer preferences, ensuring that they provide value-driven experiences. Through sentiment analysis and behavioral tracking, organizations can further refine their customer experience strategies.

Better Budget Allocation

AI helps businesses optimize marketing spend by analyzing campaign performance and identifying high-yield channels. Traditionally, marketing budgets were allocated based on past experiences or general industry trends. AI allows organizations to allocate budgets dynamically, adjusting expenditures based on real-time campaign effectiveness. By continuously monitoring return on investment (ROI), AI-driven budgeting ensures that marketing funds are directed toward strategies that yield the best results. This approach reduces unnecessary spending and improves overall financial efficiency in marketing operations.

Proactive Strategy Adjustments

Predictive analytics powered by AI enables businesses to anticipate market changes and adjust their strategies accordingly. Rather than reacting to shifts after they occur, organizations can proactively adapt their campaigns based on emerging trends. AI analyzes historical data and market conditions to forecast future scenarios, allowing businesses to stay ahead of the competition. By leveraging AI for strategy adjustments, companies can maintain relevance in dynamic markets, respond to customer demands effectively, and minimize potential risks associated with abrupt market changes.

CHALLENGES OF AI-DRIVEN DATA DECISION MAKING

Data Quality and Availability

AI models depend on well-structured, clean, and comprehensive datasets. Poor data quality, including incomplete, inconsistent, or outdated records, can lead to incorrect conclusions and ineffective strategies. Businesses need to establish data governance policies that ensure data accuracy, consistency, and accessibility. Data cleansing and validation processes should be regularly implemented to improve the quality of datasets. Additionally, organizations should integrate data from multiple reliable sources to reduce biases and gain a holistic understanding of customer behavior.

Integration with Existing Systems

Integrating AI-driven analytics with existing marketing technology (MarTech) stacks is often complex and requires a well-thought-out strategy. Businesses need to assess compatibility with their current systems and invest in scalable, flexible solutions that facilitate seamless integration. AI implementation may require upgrading legacy systems, retraining staff, and restructuring workflows. Organizations should also consider API-based solutions and cloud-based AI platforms to simplify integration and improve efficiency. Cross-departmental collaboration, including IT, marketing, and data science teams, is necessary to ensure smooth deployment and operation.

Data Privacy and Compliance

With data privacy regulations like GDPR and CCPA becoming more stringent, businesses must prioritize compliance when using AI-driven data collection and analysis. Organizations need to implement transparent data policies, obtain customer consent where necessary, and ensure robust security measures to protect sensitive information. AI systems should be designed to anonymize personal data where possible and adhere to ethical AI practices. Businesses should conduct regular compliance audits and stay informed about evolving regulations to avoid legal and reputational risks associated with mishandling data.

Interpreting AI Insights

While AI provides valuable data-driven insights, interpreting them correctly and translating them into actionable strategies remains a challenge. AI-generated recommendations must be contextualized within broader business goals and market conditions. Companies should invest in skilled data analysts who can bridge the gap between AI-generated insights and strategic decision-making. Additionally, decision-makers should be trained in data literacy to understand AI outputs effectively. Continuous testing, validation, and refinement of AI models will help businesses ensure that insights are accurate, relevant, and aligned with organizational objectives.

BEST PRACTICES FOR AI-DRIVEN DECISION MAKING

Define Clear Objectives

Before implementing AI-driven analytics, businesses should establish well-defined objectives and key performance indicators (KPIs). Clearly outlined goals help in determining what insights are needed and how they will be applied to strategic decision-making. By setting measurable benchmarks, organizations can track the effectiveness of AI applications and make necessary adjustments. Objectives should align with broader business priorities, whether they focus on enhancing customer engagement, improving sales conversions, or optimizing marketing expenses. Organizations should periodically reassess these objectives to ensure they remain relevant in evolving market conditions.

Ensure High-Quality Data

Implementing robust data governance policies is essential to maintaining data accuracy and consistency. AI models depend on structured, clean, and comprehensive datasets to generate meaningful insights. Poor-quality data, including incomplete, outdated, or inconsistent records, can lead to inaccurate predictions and ineffective strategies. Businesses should regularly audit and clean their data sources, integrating information from reliable channels. Additionally, organizations should invest in data validation tools and establish standardized protocols for data collection and management. Ensuring high-quality data is a continuous process that requires collaboration across departments.

Choose the Right AI Tools

Selecting AI solutions that align with business needs and existing systems is critical for successful integration and usability. Organizations should evaluate AI tools based on their ability to provide predictive analytics, sentiment analysis, and real-time insights. Compatibility with current marketing technology (MarTech) stacks should also be assessed to ensure seamless adoption. Businesses should consider factors such as ease of use, scalability, and vendor support when choosing AI solutions. Testing AI tools in pilot projects before full-scale implementation allows organizations to identify potential challenges and refine their strategies accordingly.

Develop Cross-Functional Collaboration

AI-driven decision-making requires collaboration between marketing, sales, and data analytics teams to maximize insights. Establishing a cross-functional team ensures that AI-generated insights are interpreted correctly and applied effectively. Marketing teams can use AI analytics to refine customer targeting strategies, while sales teams can leverage predictive insights to enhance lead conversion rates. Data analysts play a key role in translating AI findings into actionable business strategies. Regular meetings, knowledge-sharing sessions, and joint problem-solving approaches help foster collaboration across departments, enhancing the overall effectiveness of AI-driven decision-making.

Monitor and Optimize AI Models

AI models require continuous refinement and optimization to maintain accuracy and relevance in decision-making. As market conditions evolve, AI algorithms should be updated with the latest data to ensure they remain effective. Businesses should regularly evaluate AI performance, assess model outputs, and adjust algorithms as needed. Establishing monitoring frameworks allows organizations to track AI-driven recommendations and measure their impact. Additionally, businesses should stay informed about advancements in AI technology and explore opportunities to integrate new methodologies that enhance decision-making capabilities.

By following these best practices, organizations can maximize the benefits of AI-driven decision-making, ensuring that insights derived from AI analytics contribute to more effective and strategic business outcomes.

THE FUTURE OF AI IN DATA-DRIVEN MARKETING DECISIONS

AI-driven decision-making is expected to evolve further, influencing various aspects of marketing. As AI technology advances, businesses will need to adapt to new methodologies and tools that enhance decision-making capabilities. The following areas highlight the evolving role of AI in marketing:

Automated Marketing Optimization

AI is reshaping how businesses manage marketing campaigns, particularly in areas like bid adjustments, budget allocation, and ad placements. AI-powered platforms can analyze vast amounts of data in real-time, identifying the most cost-effective bidding strategies and optimizing ad performance. Through machine learning algorithms, AI assesses user interactions, past campaign data, and market trends to allocate budgets efficiently. This minimizes manual oversight, allowing marketers to focus on strategy rather than operational execution. As AI continues to improve, businesses may see further automation in A/B testing, content customization, and cross-channel campaign management, enhancing overall marketing effectiveness.

Voice and Visual Search Analytics

With the increasing use of voice assistants and image-based searches, AI-driven insights will become essential for content optimization. Businesses must refine their search engine strategies to accommodate natural language processing (NLP) and image recognition technology. AI can analyze search patterns from voice-activated devices and visual queries, helping marketers create content that aligns with these emerging behaviors. Optimizing for voice and visual searches involves structuring content in a conversational tone, implementing schema markup, and utilizing high-quality images with metadata. AI-powered analytics tools can track and predict user preferences, offering valuable insights for improving search visibility and engagement.

AI-Driven Creativity

AI is playing an increasing role in creative processes, particularly in content ideation and A/B testing. AI-driven tools can generate content recommendations based on user preferences, engagement history, and market trends. These tools assist marketers in crafting headlines, writing ad copy, and developing visually appealing graphics. A/B testing, a crucial aspect of marketing optimization, benefits from AI by enabling automated variation testing and performance tracking. AI can quickly identify which creative elements resonate most with specific audiences, allowing businesses to refine their messaging in a data-driven manner. As AI-generated content becomes more sophisticated, companies can strike a balance between automation and human creativity to ensure authenticity and relevance.

Advanced Personalization Models

AI enables businesses to provide real-time, highly personalized customer experience. By analyzing customer interactions across multiple touchpoints, AI can predict user preferences and deliver relevant content at the right moment. Personalization extends beyond product recommendations—it includes customized email campaigns, adaptive website experiences, and dynamic pricing strategies. AI-driven customer segmentation helps businesses tailor their communication based on behavioral insights, improving engagement and conversion rates. As machine learning models evolve, personalization will become even more refined, with AI-driven interactions mirroring human-like adaptability to consumer needs.

By embracing these advancements, businesses can refine their AI-driven marketing strategies, enhancing efficiency, engagement, and adaptability in an ever-evolving digital landscape.

AI has significantly enhanced data-driven decision-making by enabling businesses to analyze vast amounts of data, identify patterns, and optimize marketing strategies with greater precision. Through predictive analytics, sentiment analysis, and real-time data processing, AI helps marketers refine customer targeting, personalize content, and allocate budgets more effectively. These capabilities allow businesses to shift from intuition-based decision-making to more structured, data-backed strategies that improve engagement and campaign performance.

Despite its advantages, AI-driven decision-making comes with challenges such as data quality management, system integration, and compliance with data privacy regulations. Businesses must ensure that AI models are trained on accurate, unbiased data and are continuously monitored for performance and relevance. Additionally, human oversight remains essential to interpret AI-generated insights in the right context and align them with broader business goals.

As AI technology evolves, emerging trends such as automated marketing optimization, voice and visual search analytics, and advanced personalization models will further refine marketing strategies. Organizations that adopt AI thoughtfully—by prioritizing data integrity, ethical considerations, and ongoing optimization—will be better positioned to make informed decisions that enhance customer experiences and drive meaningful results in an increasingly digital marketplace.

Key Takeaways

- AI enhances data-driven decision-making by analyzing customer behavior, predicting trends, and optimizing marketing strategies.
- Key AI-driven analytics include customer behavior analysis, predictive analytics, sentiment analysis, marketing attribution, and real-time data processing.
- AI improves marketing accuracy, speeds up decision-making, enhances customer experience, and optimizes budget allocation.
- Challenges such as data quality, system integration, and compliance with data privacy regulations must be managed for successful AI implementation.
- The future of AI in data-driven marketing includes automated marketing optimization, voice and visual search analytics, AI-driven creativity, and advanced personalization models.

Reflection Questions

- How does your business currently use data in marketing decisions?
- What areas of your marketing strategy could benefit from AI-driven analytics?
- How can AI improve customer engagement and personalization in your marketing efforts?
- What steps can your organization take to ensure compliance with data privacy regulations while using AI?

Action Steps

- Identify key marketing areas where AI-driven decision-making could improve accuracy and efficiency.
- Research AI tools that align with your business needs, such as predictive analytics or sentiment analysis platforms.
- Evaluate the quality of your data and implement processes for regular data validation and cleansing.
- Conduct a small-scale test of AI-powered analytics in a specific campaign to measure its impact.
- Establish a framework for ongoing monitoring and optimization of AI-driven marketing decisions.

MODULE 6
PERSONALIZATION AT SCALE USING AI AND MARTECH

The power of hyper personalization cannot be overlooked, as it plays a crucial role in creating meaningful customer experiences. This chapter delves into the role of AI in personalization, the technologies that enable it, strategies for implementation, challenges faced, and emerging trends that will shape the future of AI-powered marketing personalization.

THE ROLE OF AI IN PERSONALIZATION

AI enhances personalization by processing vast amounts of data, identifying patterns, and delivering customized content, recommendations, and interactions based on user preferences and behaviors. Marketers can harness AI to:

- **Understand customer intent** through in-depth behavioral and sentiment analysis, identifying patterns that indicate preferences, needs, and future actions. This allows businesses to tailor their approach and provide relevant content, offers, and recommendations to customers at the right time.
- **Deliver personalized content** tailored to an individual's needs and preferences by dynamically adjusting messaging, visuals, and recommendations based on past interactions and engagement metrics. This ensures that customers receive content that aligns with their interests, increasing the likelihood of engagement and conversion.
- **Automate customer interactions** across multiple channels,

ensuring seamless engagement through AI-driven chatbots, automated email campaigns, and intelligent response systems. By leveraging AI for automation, businesses can maintain consistency in customer interactions while optimizing efficiency and response time.

- **Optimize marketing campaigns** based on real-time data insights, allowing businesses to refine their strategies and improve the effectiveness of their outreach efforts. AI helps analyze engagement data, customer feedback, and performance metrics to adjust messaging, timing, and content for better results.
- **Improve customer retention** through targeted messaging and loyalty programs that reward customer engagement and foster long-term relationships. AI-driven segmentation enables businesses to identify at-risk customers and implement re-engagement strategies to keep them connected to the brand.

By integrating AI into their personalization strategies, businesses can provide value-driven, individualized experiences that foster stronger customer relationships and improve overall marketing efficiency.

KEY AI-POWERED PERSONALIZATION TECHNIQUES

Dynamic Content Customization

AI-powered platforms enable dynamic content generation by adjusting website elements, email content, and product recommendations in real-time based on user behavior. Examples include:

- **Personalized landing pages** that adapt based on browsing history and purchase behavior.

- **AI-driven product recommendations** that cater to users' preferences and past purchases.
- **Automated messaging adjustments** based on a customer's lifecycle stage, improving relevance.

Dynamic content customization plays a crucial role in improving user engagement by making digital experiences more relevant. For example, when a user visits an e-commerce site, the homepage may change dynamically based on previous browsing activity. If a customer has recently searched for running shoes, the homepage may highlight new arrivals in running footwear or offer discounts on similar products. This level of customization helps businesses provide timely, context-aware interactions that align with user intent.

Beyond websites, AI-driven content customization extends to email marketing and mobile applications. Emails can include product recommendations tailored to individual users, ensuring higher open rates and engagement. Similarly, mobile apps can personalize the user interface, adjusting displayed categories and suggested content based on real-time user actions.

Predictive Personalization

AI algorithms predict customer needs and behaviors by analyzing previous interactions, helping businesses:

- **Identify the most relevant products or services** for each user.
- **Optimize email timing** for improved engagement and conversion.
- **Detect potential customer churn** and deploy re-engagement strategies to retain users.

Predictive personalization enables marketers to anticipate customer behavior before it happens. By leveraging machine learning models, businesses can analyze purchasing trends, browsing habits, and engagement history to predict what a customer might do next. For instance, an AI system may recognize that a customer typically purchases skincare products every six weeks and can trigger an automated reminder email with a replenishment offer just before the expected purchase date.

Another application of predictive personalization is in content delivery. Streaming services use predictive algorithms to suggest shows or movies based on viewing history. These models take into account watch patterns, search behavior, and even the time of day when users typically watch content, helping create a more tailored experience.

Beyond individual users, predictive personalization also benefits businesses by helping them allocate marketing resources effectively. Instead of sending blanket promotions to all users, AI can identify high-value customers who are likely to respond positively to targeted offers, optimizing marketing spend and increasing return on investment.

Behavior-Based Email Personalization

AI enhances email marketing by dynamically segmenting audiences and personalizing content. This involves:

- **Triggering automated emails** based on customer actions (e.g., abandoned carts, completed purchases).
- **Personalizing subject lines and email content** based on past engagement.
- **Optimizing email send times** using AI analysis for increased open and click rates.

Behavior-based email personalization ensures that marketing messages are timely and relevant. For instance, if a customer adds items to their cart but does not complete the purchase, an automated email can be sent with a gentle reminder or an incentive, such as free shipping, to encourage conversion.

AI can also refine email personalization by analyzing how recipients engage with previous messages. If a customer consistently opens promotional emails in the evening, future emails can be scheduled to arrive at that time for maximum engagement. Additionally, subject lines and messaging can be adjusted dynamically to align with what a customer finds most appealing based on their past interactions.

Beyond individual emails, AI-driven email campaigns can include personalized drip sequences. These automated workflows guide users through a series of emails designed to educate, engage, and ultimately convert them. Each step in the sequence is personalized based on user actions, ensuring a relevant and non-intrusive customer experience.

Conversational AI and Chatbots

AI-driven chatbots and virtual assistants provide personalized support by:

- **Delivering tailored product suggestions** based on previous interactions.
- **Answering frequently asked questions** with contextually relevant responses.
- **Providing real-time support** through natural language processing (NLP), reducing the need for human intervention.

Chatbots powered by AI enhance customer support and sales interactions by delivering personalized responses in real-time. Instead of generic replies, chatbots use historical data to understand customer preferences and provide tailored recommendations. For example, an online clothing retailer's chatbot can suggest outfits based on past purchases, ensuring relevance in customer interactions.

These AI-powered assistants also play a crucial role in customer service. By analyzing frequently asked questions and previous interactions, chatbots can respond with appropriate solutions, helping customers find the information they need without requiring human assistance. Moreover, for complex inquiries, chatbots can seamlessly escalate the conversation to human agents, maintaining efficiency while preserving a personal touch.

Voice-based AI assistants, such as those integrated into smart devices, also enhance conversational experiences by providing personalized recommendations. Whether it is a voice assistant suggesting a restaurant based on dining history or an AI-powered home automation system adjusting settings based on past preferences, conversational AI is shaping the future of user interaction.

AI-Powered Customer Segmentation

AI-driven segmentation refines audience targeting by analyzing behavioral data instead of relying solely on demographics. Benefits include:

- **More precise targeting** for digital advertising campaigns.
- **Enhanced loyalty program recommendations** tailored to customer preferences.
- **Improved messaging relevance** across multiple marketing channels.

Traditional segmentation often relies on broad demographic data, such as age and location, which can overlook behavioral nuances. AI-powered segmentation, however, takes a more data-driven approach, grouping users based on their interactions, preferences, and purchasing habits. This allows marketers to create highly specific customer segments that receive personalized offers and messaging.

For example, an AI system can identify a group of users who frequently browse but do not purchase, triggering targeted ads with limited-time discounts. Similarly, AI-driven segmentation can enhance loyalty programs by identifying high-value customers and offering them exclusive rewards or personalized promotions.

By refining audience segmentation, businesses can improve marketing efficiency and customer satisfaction, ensuring that each user receives relevant content tailored to their needs.

IMPLEMENTING AI-DRIVEN PERSONALIZATION

Personalization has become an essential aspect of modern marketing, helping brands create customized experiences that resonate with individual customers. AI and marketing technology (MarTech) empower businesses to implement personalization at scale, ensuring that tailored interactions reach the right audience at the right time. Through advanced data analysis and automation, AI-driven personalization enables companies to enhance engagement, drive conversions, and build stronger customer relationships.

Collecting and Analyzing Data Effectively

Successful AI-driven personalization relies on high-quality data. Businesses should:

- **Aggregate data** from multiple touchpoints (web, mobile, social media, CRM systems, etc.). Gathering data from various sources ensures a comprehensive understanding of customer behavior. This includes browsing history, purchase patterns, engagement metrics, and feedback collected across different channels. The integration of these data points allows businesses to create a more accurate profile of each customer, enabling personalized experiences.
- **Ensure data accuracy and consistency** to avoid incorrect insights and recommendations. Inaccurate or inconsistent data can lead to misleading conclusions and ineffective personalization efforts. Businesses must implement data

validation techniques, regular audits, and cleansing processes to maintain data quality. Using automated AI tools, companies can detect and correct inconsistencies, ensuring that the data used for personalization remains reliable.

- **Leverage AI-powered analytics tools** to derive actionable insights from collected data. AI-powered analytics tools help organizations make sense of vast amounts of information. These tools use machine learning algorithms to identify trends, uncover correlations, and generate predictive insights. By leveraging AI-driven data analysis, businesses can refine their marketing strategies and provide more relevant recommendations to their customers.

Choosing the Right Personalization Tools

There are several AI-driven personalization tools available, including:

Customer Data Platforms (CDPs): Unify customer data for more effective personalization. CDPs allow businesses to create a unified customer profile by consolidating data from various sources. This centralized approach enhances the ability to deliver seamless personalized experiences across multiple channels. CDPs also facilitate real-time data updates, ensuring that personalization efforts are based on the latest customer interactions.

AI Recommendation Engines: Provide tailored product and content recommendations. AI-powered recommendation engines analyze customer behavior, preferences, and purchase history to suggest relevant products, services, or content. These engines enhance customer experience by offering timely and contextually appropriate suggestions, which can increase engagement and conversion rates.

Marketing Automation Software: Automate personalized messaging across channels. Marketing automation tools streamline the delivery of personalized communications by automating email campaigns, push notifications, and social media interactions. These tools help businesses engage with customers at the right moment, based on their actions and preferences, without requiring constant manual intervention.

Testing and Optimization

AI personalization should be continuously tested and refined. Best practices include:

- **A/B testing** to compare different personalization strategies. A/B testing involves running controlled experiments where different personalization techniques are tested to determine their effectiveness. By comparing engagement rates, conversion metrics, and customer feedback, businesses can identify the most impactful personalization strategies and make data-driven decisions.
- **Adjusting messaging and targeting** based on AI-generated insights. AI tools analyze customer responses to personalized content and provide insights into which messages resonate the most. Businesses can use these insights to refine their messaging, ensuring that their communications align with customer interests and behaviors.
- **Tracking engagement metrics** to enhance content relevance and impact. Monitoring engagement metrics such as click-through rates, time spent on site, and conversion rates helps businesses assess the effectiveness of their personalization efforts. AI-powered analytics tools can track these metrics in real-time and provide recommendations for adjustments to improve content relevance.

Privacy and Data Compliance

With increasing concerns about data privacy, businesses must adhere to regulations by:

- **Providing transparency** regarding data collection and usage. Businesses must clearly communicate how customer data is collected, stored, and used. Providing detailed privacy policies and consent options helps build trust and ensures compliance with data protection regulations.
- **Allowing customers to manage their personalization preferences.** Offering customers the ability to control how their data is used for personalization enhances trust and compliance. Businesses can implement preference management tools that allow users to opt in or out of specific types of personalized experiences.
- **Implementing security measures** to protect sensitive customer data. Data breaches and unauthorized access can erode customer trust and lead to regulatory penalties. Businesses should implement strong security measures, such as encryption, access controls, and regular security audits, to safeguard customer data.

CHALLENGES OF AI-DRIVEN PERSONALIZATION

Data Privacy and Consumer Trust

Consumers are becoming more conscious of data privacy. To build trust, businesses must implement comprehensive measures that ensure transparency, data control, and adherence to privacy laws.

- **Clearly communicate** how customer data is used by providing detailed explanations of privacy policies and using clear, concise messaging. Businesses should inform customers of data collection methods, the purpose of data usage, and how personalization benefits them.
- **Offer opt-in and opt-out choices** for personalized experiences. Providing users with control over their data fosters trust. Businesses can implement easily accessible preference settings where customers can manage their personalization preferences.

- **Ensure compliance** with global data protection regulations such as GDPR, CCPA, and other relevant privacy laws. Organizations should regularly review policies and update their compliance frameworks to align with evolving regulations.
- **Implement strong security measures** to protect customer data. Encryption, secure access controls, and robust cybersecurity protocols must be in place to prevent breaches and unauthorized data access.
- **Educate customers on data privacy** by sharing information on safe online practices and how businesses handle their data securely. Transparency initiatives, such as privacy dashboards, can also help customers feel more confident about their data security.

Balancing Automation and Human Touch

While AI enhances efficiency, over-reliance on automation can make customer interactions feel impersonal. To address this, businesses should integrate AI with human interaction where needed to maintain authenticity and customer satisfaction.

- **Incorporate human intervention** where complex interactions require empathy. AI can handle repetitive tasks, but customer service teams should intervene when nuanced understanding and decision-making are needed.
- **Blend AI with customer service teams** for a more natural experience. AI-powered chatbots should have seamless handoffs to human agents for cases requiring deeper engagement. Training employees on AI insights and recommendations can further enhance customer interactions.
- **Customize AI-driven interactions** to ensure that automated messages align with brand voice and customer preferences. AI-powered personalization should feel natural rather than robotic, making interactions more engaging.

- **Gather customer feedback** to understand their experience with AI interactions. By listening to user concerns and adjusting automation strategies accordingly, businesses can improve the balance between automation and human touch.

Integration with Existing MarTech Systems

Implementing AI-driven personalization requires seamless integration with existing systems, which can be complex. Businesses should take strategic steps to ensure smooth implementation and interoperability.

- **Invest in AI-compatible MarTech solutions.** Choosing technology that integrates well with existing platforms reduces disruption and maximizes the potential of AI-driven personalization.
- **Ensure proper API connectivity** between platforms to facilitate data sharing and real-time updates. A well-integrated system enables more accurate personalization across channels.
- **Train teams** on AI tools for effective adoption. Employees must understand how to use AI-driven insights and automation tools to enhance customer engagement strategies.
- **Conduct regular audits** to assess how AI personalization is functioning within the MarTech stack. Identifying areas for improvement can help businesses refine their approach and optimize efficiency.

Ensuring AI Accuracy and Relevance

AI models must be continuously trained and refined to ensure accurate recommendations. This involves:

- **Regularly updating AI models** with fresh data. Customer preferences and behaviors change over time, so AI models must be trained on the latest information to remain relevant.

- **Monitoring AI-generated recommendations** for effectiveness. Businesses should analyze performance metrics, such as engagement rates and customer feedback, to assess the accuracy of AI-driven personalization.
- **Eliminating biases** in AI-driven personalization strategies. AI models should be evaluated for potential biases that may affect recommendations. Businesses must ensure that their AI tools do not inadvertently reinforce stereotypes or exclude certain customer groups.
- **Establishing human oversight** in AI decision-making. Although AI automates personalization, human review is necessary to ensure ethical and effective personalization.
- **Testing personalization strategies** using A/B testing and other methods. Experimenting with different AI-driven recommendations helps businesses refine their approach and improve accuracy.

By addressing these challenges with structured strategies, businesses can leverage AI-driven personalization effectively while maintaining trust, compliance, and meaningful customer relationships.

FUTURE TRENDS IN AI-POWERED PERSONALIZATION

AI-Powered Hyper-Personalization

AI advancements will enable deeper personalization by considering real-time intent, external factors, and contextual insights.

Hyper-personalization involves leveraging data beyond traditional user behaviors, including contextual information such as real-time location, weather conditions, device usage, and even mood analysis. By incorporating these dynamic elements, businesses can create highly relevant experiences tailored to the individual. For example, an AI-powered retail application might adjust recommendations based on a customer's location, suggesting warm clothing if they are in a colder region or swimwear if they are near a beach destination.

Another key aspect of AI-driven hyper-personalization is adaptive learning. Unlike static personalization models, AI continuously refines recommendations based on immediate feedback. If a customer regularly skips a particular type of content or product, the system will adjust accordingly, reducing irrelevant suggestions over time. Furthermore, AI-powered hyper-personalization will expand beyond traditional digital interactions into real-world experiences, such as in-store recommendations and AI-assisted shopping guides tailored to user preferences.

Personalization in Voice and Visual Search

With the rise of voice assistants and visual search, AI-driven personalization will move beyond text-based recommendations to include:

Voice-activated shopping experience | Voice commerce is becoming increasingly prevalent, with AI-driven assistants like Alexa and Google Assistant enabling hands-free shopping. Users can receive tailored recommendations based on previous orders, preferences, and spoken queries. Businesses can optimize their product listings and customer interactions for voice search, ensuring that AI understands and responds effectively to conversational commands.

Image-based product discovery | Visual search enables users to upload images or take photos to find similar products. AI can analyze visual patterns, colors, and shapes to offer accurate product matches. Retailers are integrating AI-powered visual search tools to help customers find the exact item they are looking for without relying solely on keywords. This is particularly useful in fashion, home decor, and automotive industries, where visuals play a significant role in purchasing decisions.

AI-driven content adjustments for various search modes | AI can dynamically adjust search results based on user context. For instance, if a person frequently uses voice search at home, their recommendations may focus on entertainment and household products, whereas visual search queries made on the go might prioritize fashion or travel-related suggestions. AI's ability to process and adapt to different modes of interaction will lead to a more intuitive and natural search experience.

AI-Generated Personalized Content

AI will play a greater role in content creation by dynamically generating variations of text, visuals, and layouts to align with individual preferences.

AI-powered content generation tools can create tailored marketing messages, advertisements, and even website copy based on a user's profile and preferences. These tools use natural language processing (NLP) and machine learning to craft personalized content that resonates with the reader. For example, AI can generate product descriptions that highlight the most relevant features for different customer segments, ensuring that each user sees a version of the content most suited to their interests.

Additionally, AI-driven design tools enable the personalization of website layouts and mobile app interfaces. By analyzing user behavior, AI can modify the placement of elements, adjust color schemes, and suggest content arrangements that improve engagement. For example, an e-commerce site might display different homepage designs based on whether a visitor is a frequent shopper or a first-time user, ensuring a more relevant browsing experience.

AI-generated video content is another emerging trend, where AI tools can create short, personalized video ads tailored to specific audiences. These videos can incorporate dynamic text, images, and voiceovers that align with a user's interests and demographics. As AI-generated content evolves, businesses will be able to scale personalization efforts while maintaining high levels of engagement and relevance.

Ethical AI in Personalization

Future personalization efforts will focus on ethical AI practices, ensuring:

Fairness in recommendation algorithms | AI must be designed to minimize biases and ensure that recommendations are inclusive and diverse. Businesses should regularly audit their AI models to identify and eliminate any unintended biases in content recommendations, hiring algorithms, and personalized marketing campaigns.

Transparency in AI decision-making | Consumers are increasingly concerned about how AI makes decisions regarding their data and recommendations. To address this, businesses must provide clear explanations of how AI-driven personalization works. This can include offering transparency reports, explainable AI models, and customer-friendly explanations of why certain products or content are being recommended.

Elimination of unintended biases in personalized content delivery | AI models trained on historical data can sometimes reinforce existing biases, leading to skewed recommendations. Companies need to use diverse training data sets and implement fairness-checking mechanisms to prevent discriminatory practices. Ethical AI frameworks should be established to guide AI deployment in personalization efforts, ensuring fairness and accountability.

Beyond fairness and transparency, ethical AI personalization also involves respecting user privacy and consent. AI should only use data that users have explicitly agreed to share, and businesses should offer clear options for users to control their personalization settings. Striking the right balance between personalization and privacy will be key to maintaining consumer trust.

AI-driven personalization is transforming marketing by enabling businesses to deliver relevant and tailored experiences at scale. By leveraging AI-powered tools, companies can analyze customer data, predict behaviors, and automate interactions, making marketing efforts more precise and effective. Techniques such as dynamic content customization, predictive personalization, behavior-based email marketing, conversational AI, and AI-powered segmentation help brands engage customers with greater relevance across multiple channels.

However, successful implementation requires addressing challenges such as data privacy, balancing automation with human interaction, and ensuring AI-driven recommendations remain accurate and unbiased. Businesses must adopt ethical AI practices, provide transparency in personalization efforts, and maintain consumer trust by allowing users control over their data and preferences.

Looking ahead, advancements in hyper-personalization, voice and visual search, AI-generated content, and ethical AI frameworks will further refine how brands connect with customers. Organizations that strategically integrate AI-driven personalization while prioritizing data security, compliance, and continuous optimization will be well-positioned to enhance engagement and build lasting customer relationships in an increasingly digital landscape.

Key Takeaways

- AI enables businesses to implement personalization at scale by analyzing customer behavior, predicting preferences, and automating content delivery.
- AI-driven personalization techniques include dynamic content customization, predictive personalization, behavior-based email marketing, conversational AI, and AI-powered customer segmentation.
- Implementing AI-driven personalization requires high-quality data collection, the right MarTech tools, continuous testing, and a strong focus on data privacy and compliance.
- Challenges such as balancing automation with human interaction must be addressed for effective AI personalization.
- Emerging trends in AI-powered personalization include hyper-personalization, AI-generated content, and ethical AI frameworks.

Reflection Questions

- How does your business currently personalize customer interactions?
- How can predictive personalization enhance customer engagement in your marketing strategy?
- How can you balance automation with human oversight in customer interactions?

Action Steps

- Evaluate your current personalization strategies and identify areas where AI can enhance targeting and content delivery.
- Research AI-driven MarTech tools, such as CDPs and recommendation engines, to support your personalization initiatives.
- Improve data collection processes to ensure high-quality, real-time insights that enable more accurate personalization.
- Test AI-driven personalization techniques, such as predictive product recommendations and automated customer segmentation.
- Establish a framework for ethical AI usage, ensuring transparency, compliance, and fairness in AI-driven marketing personalization.

MODULE 7 AI-DRIVEN CUSTOMER SEGMENTATION AND TARGETING

Customer segmentation and targeting are fundamental aspects of marketing strategy, allowing businesses to group audiences based on shared characteristics and behaviors. Traditional methods of segmentation have relied on demographic data, consumer surveys, and limited behavioral insights. However, with the advent of artificial intelligence (AI), businesses can now process vast amounts of data efficiently, identify intricate patterns, and predict customer behavior with greater accuracy.

AI-driven customer segmentation and targeting improve marketing efficiency by enabling businesses to craft personalized experiences, optimize ad spend, and automate marketing strategies in real-time. This chapter explores the transformative impact of AI in customer segmentation and targeting, delves into key techniques, outlines implementation strategies, examines challenges, and provides insights into future trends shaping this domain.

THE ROLE OF AI IN CUSTOMER SEGMENTATION AND TARGETING

AI has transformed customer segmentation by moving beyond traditional methodologies and incorporating behavioral, psychographic, and predictive insights. Businesses can leverage AI-driven segmentation to:

Identifying Micro-Segments Based on Engagement Patterns

AI enables marketers to move beyond broad audience categorizations by identifying micro-segments within their customer base. By analyzing interaction data, machine learning models can detect patterns that define smaller, highly specific customer groups. These segments can be based on:

- Browsing behavior and purchase history.
- Frequency and timing of interactions with digital platforms.
- Product preferences and category affinities.

Micro-segmentation helps businesses tailor marketing efforts with increased precision, ensuring that customers receive messages and promotions relevant to their behavior and interests. This approach leads to higher engagement rates and improves the overall effectiveness of marketing campaigns.

Optimizing Ad Targeting for Higher Conversion Rates

AI enhances ad targeting by analyzing large-scale consumer data and predicting which audiences are most likely to convert. Businesses can optimize their advertising strategies by:

- Identifying lookalike audiences that share characteristics with high-value customers.
- Adjusting ad placements dynamically based on engagement metrics.
- Personalizing ad creatives based on individual preferences.

By leveraging AI-driven targeting, businesses can maximize the efficiency of their marketing budgets, reducing wasted ad spend and improving return on investment (ROI). AI also enables real-time ad optimizations, ensuring that campaigns are continuously refined based on performance data.

Enhancing Customer Experiences Through Personalized Messaging

One of the most impactful uses of AI in segmentation is delivering highly personalized marketing messages. AI analyzes:

- Previous interactions with emails, advertisements, and customer support.
- Sentiment analysis from reviews and feedback.
- Preferred communication channels and content types.

With these insights, businesses can send messages that resonate with individual customers, improving engagement rates and fostering brand loyalty. AI also allows for adaptive messaging, where campaigns evolve based on ongoing interactions, keeping marketing efforts relevant over time.

Automating the Segmentation Process for Real-Time Updates

Traditional segmentation methods require manual adjustments based on observed trends. AI-driven segmentation automates this process, updating customer segments in real time based on new data. Key automation features include:

- Continuous learning from user interactions and adjusting customer categories accordingly.
- Identifying seasonal shifts in consumer behavior and adapting marketing efforts.
- Recognizing lifecycle stages, such as onboarding, engagement, and churn risk, and tailoring strategies accordingly.

By integrating AI into segmentation and targeting, businesses can make more informed decisions, reduce wasted marketing spend, and create impactful customer interactions. This dynamic approach ensures that businesses stay relevant and competitive in an ever-changing marketplace.

KEY AI-POWERED CUSTOMER SEGMENTATION TECHNIQUES

AI-powered segmentation techniques leverage machine learning and data analytics to categorize customers more effectively. Below are the key techniques businesses use to enhance targeting and personalization:

Demographic and Geographic Segmentation

Demographic and geographic segmentation have long been foundational in marketing, but AI enhances their accuracy by integrating behavioral insights. Businesses can now refine audience segments based on:

- Age, gender, income, and education levels.
- Geographic location, cultural preferences, and seasonal shopping trends.
- Localized demand patterns and regional economic conditions.

AI enables deeper analysis, identifying subtle correlations that manual segmentation may overlook. For example, AI can assess how purchasing behaviors vary by region and demographic group, helping brands refine their product positioning and marketing strategies accordingly.

Behavioral Segmentation

Behavioral segmentation categorizes customers based on their interactions with a brand. AI algorithms process large datasets to detect behavioral patterns such as:

- Purchase history, transaction frequency, and average order value.
- Website interactions, including time spent on pages, bounce rates, and browsing history.

- Engagement with marketing emails, paid advertisements, and social media content.

By analyzing behavioral data, businesses can predict customer intent, deliver relevant recommendations, and optimize their marketing efforts for different consumer groups.

Psychographic Segmentation

Psychographic segmentation involves analyzing customer attitudes, interests, values, and lifestyles. AI facilitates this by processing:

- Social media activity and sentiment analysis.
- Survey responses and customer feedback.
- Online forum discussions and content preferences.

This type of segmentation is particularly useful for brands looking to establish emotional connections with customers by aligning their messaging with consumer values and preferences.

Predictive Segmentation

Predictive segmentation uses machine learning algorithms to anticipate future customer behaviors based on historical data. Businesses can leverage AI to:

- Identify high-value customers who are likely to make repeat purchases.
- Detect customers at risk of churning and implement retention strategies.
- Optimize marketing offers based on predicted buying intent.

Predictive segmentation enables businesses to be proactive rather than reactive, enhancing customer retention and lifetime value.

Real-Time Dynamic Segmentation

Unlike static segmentation, real-time dynamic segmentation updates customer profiles automatically based on:

- Changes in browsing and purchasing behavior.
- Seasonal trends and market fluctuations.
- Customer lifecycle stages, such as onboarding, retention, or churn risk.

AI-driven dynamic segmentation ensures that businesses can adapt their marketing strategies in real-time, delivering personalized experiences that evolve with customer preferences.

IMPLEMENTING AI-DRIVEN SEGMENTATION AND TARGETING

Successful implementation of AI-driven segmentation requires structured planning and the right tools. The following steps outline the process:

Collecting and Structuring Data

AI-driven segmentation relies on comprehensive data collection from multiple sources, including:

- Customer relationship management (CRM) systems.
- Website analytics and behavioral tracking tools.
- Social media interactions and engagement metrics.
- Transaction history and loyalty program data.

To ensure the data serves its intended purpose, businesses must focus on the accuracy, consistency, and completeness of the data collected. AI models depend on high-quality data inputs; otherwise, their predictive capabilities and recommendations could be flawed. Cleaning data, removing duplicate records, and validating input sources are critical steps before leveraging AI for segmentation.

Businesses must also ensure data structuring. Organizing data into meaningful categories improves the efficiency of AI-driven segmentation. AI systems work best when datasets are well-formatted, categorized, and labeled. Structured data allows algorithms to process information effectively, uncovering patterns and insights more quickly.

Furthermore, businesses should integrate data from multiple touchpoints to create a unified customer profile. Combining CRM data with website interactions and transaction history ensures a more comprehensive view of consumer behavior. AI can then analyze this unified dataset to derive deeper insights that inform marketing strategies.

Choosing AI Tools for Segmentation

Businesses can implement AI-driven segmentation using various tools, such as:

- **Customer Data Platforms (CDPs):** Aggregate and unify customer data from multiple touchpoints.
- **AI-Powered Analytics Tools:** Process large datasets to uncover segmentation opportunities.
- **Marketing Automation Platforms:** Execute targeted campaigns based on AI-driven insights.

Selecting the right tools depends on several factors, including the business's goals, budget, and technical capabilities. Some platforms specialize in specific aspects of AI-driven segmentation, while others provide an end-to-end solution.

AI tools should seamlessly integrate with existing marketing and CRM systems to avoid disruptions. Compatibility ensures smooth data flow across platforms, preventing data silos that could hinder segmentation accuracy. Businesses should evaluate tools based on their interoperability with existing software infrastructure.

Scalability is another consideration when selecting AI tools. As businesses grow, their data volume and segmentation complexity will increase. AI tools must be capable of handling larger datasets and evolving segmentation needs without requiring frequent replacements or overhauls.

Businesses should also consider the ease of use and implementation effort required for each AI tool. Some platforms require significant technical expertise, while others offer user-friendly interfaces with drag-and-drop functionalities. Choosing a tool that aligns with internal capabilities can improve adoption and efficiency.

Applying AI to Personalize Marketing Campaigns

After segmentation, AI optimizes targeting by:

- Personalizing ad creative, messaging, and offers.
- Adjusting email marketing strategies to suit different audience segments.
- Refining content marketing based on segment-specific preferences.

AI enables businesses to deliver tailored marketing campaigns that resonate with customers on an individual level. By analyzing past interactions and customer preferences, AI-powered marketing platforms can dynamically adjust messaging, offers, and content to suit each segment.

Personalization extends beyond marketing communication to product recommendations, website experiences, and chatbot interactions. AI-driven personalization ensures that each customer experiences a relevant and engaging interaction with the brand, increasing engagement and conversion rates.

Businesses can also use AI to automate customer journey mapping, predicting the next best action for each segment. AI identifies where customers are on their journey, whether they are new visitors, engaged prospects, or repeat buyers, and delivers tailored content accordingly. This approach increases the likelihood of guiding customers toward conversion.

AI-powered personalization should be continuously refined through testing and feedback loops. Businesses should track engagement rates, open rates, and click-through rates to determine the effectiveness of personalized campaigns. AI can analyze this performance data and adjust targeting strategies in real-time.

Measuring and Optimizing AI-Driven Segmentation

Continuous evaluation is essential to maintain segmentation accuracy. Businesses should:

- Track engagement and conversion rates across different segments.
- Conduct A/B testing on targeted campaigns.
- Use AI insights to refine audience segmentation strategies over time.

Measuring the success of AI-driven segmentation involves monitoring key performance indicators (KPIs). Businesses should track how each segment responds to marketing efforts, evaluating metrics such as conversion rates, engagement levels, and return on ad spend (ROAS).

A/B testing plays a crucial role in optimization. By experimenting with different messages, offers, and content variations, businesses can determine which approaches resonate best with each segment. AI can analyze A/B testing results and suggest improvements for future campaigns.

AI-driven segmentation should also be continuously refined based on real-time data. Customer behaviors change over time, and AI algorithms should adapt accordingly. Businesses should regularly review segmentation models, ensuring they remain relevant and effective.

Another aspect of optimization involves feedback loops. AI systems learn from new data and adjust segmentation rules based on customer interactions. Businesses can leverage AI-driven insights to enhance audience segmentation strategies and maintain high relevance in their marketing efforts.

By following these steps, ensuring data quality, selecting the right AI tools, applying personalized marketing strategies, and continuously optimizing segmentation—businesses can effectively implement AI-driven segmentation and targeting. This structured approach allows businesses to create meaningful customer experiences, maximize marketing efficiency, and drive higher engagement and conversion rates.

CHALLENGES OF AI-DRIVEN SEGMENTATION AND TARGETING

Despite its advantages, AI-driven segmentation presents certain challenges that businesses must address to maximize its effectiveness.

Data Quality and Availability

AI models require high-quality data for accurate segmentation. Incomplete, outdated, or inconsistent data can lead to misleading insights, reducing the effectiveness of AI-driven targeting. Businesses must ensure proper data governance by implementing measures such as:

- Regular data audits to identify and rectify inaccuracies.
- Standardized data collection processes to maintain consistency across sources.
- Integration of multiple data streams to enhance the completeness of customer profiles.

Additionally, organizations should invest in data cleansing tools and AI models capable of handling missing or ambiguous data to improve segmentation accuracy.

Integration with Existing Systems

Ensuring AI segmentation tools work seamlessly with CRM, analytics, and marketing automation platforms can be complex and require technical expertise. Businesses often face challenges such as:

- Legacy system incompatibilities that hinder data synchronization.
- The need for API connections and middleware to facilitate smooth data transfer.
- Organizational resistance to adopting new AI-driven processes.

To address these issues, companies should develop a structured integration plan, work with IT specialists, and gradually implement AI tools while ensuring minimal disruption to existing workflows.

Privacy and Compliance Issues

AI-driven segmentation must align with data privacy regulations such as GDPR and CCPA to ensure customer data is protected and ethically used. Compliance-related challenges include:

- Obtaining explicit user consent for data collection and processing.
- Ensuring data anonymization and encryption to prevent unauthorized access.
- Adhering to jurisdiction-specific privacy laws when handling global customer data.

Businesses should implement transparent data policies, provide clear opt-in and opt-out options, and regularly update their compliance strategies to align with evolving legal frameworks.

Over-Reliance on Automation

While AI improves segmentation accuracy, excessive reliance on automation without human oversight can lead to unintended consequences. Some risks include:

- AI misinterpreting consumer behaviors and creating inaccurate segments.
- Ethical concerns regarding bias in AI-driven targeting decisions.
- Reduced ability to adapt to nuanced customer needs that require human judgment.

To mitigate these risks, organizations should maintain a balance between automation and human oversight. Regularly reviewing AI-generated segments, incorporating qualitative insights, and maintaining a customer-first approach ensure ethical and effective AI-driven segmentation strategies.

FUTURE TRENDS IN AI-POWERED SEGMENTATION AND TARGETING

As AI technology advances, new trends are shaping customer segmentation and targeting:

Hyper-Personalized Marketing

AI is enhancing real-time micro-segmentation, allowing businesses to deliver highly tailored experiences at scale. Unlike broad segmentation strategies, hyper-personalized marketing dynamically adjusts content, recommendations, and engagement strategies based on real-time user behavior. By leveraging machine learning models, businesses can analyze historical interactions and predict future customer preferences. This allows for:

- Adaptive content strategies where website interfaces, email campaigns, and advertisements change in response to customer engagement.
- Real-time offer customization, presenting users with relevant promotions based on their behavior.
- Enhanced customer journey mapping, ensuring that each step in the consumer lifecycle is addressed with precision.

Hyper-personalization ensures that marketing remains relevant to the consumer, fostering stronger engagement and higher conversion rates.

AI-Driven Sentiment Analysis

AI-powered sentiment analysis is reshaping targeting strategies by examining customer emotions and opinions across multiple channels, including social media, reviews, and customer service interactions. This method allows businesses to:

- Gauge public perception of a brand, product, or service in real time.
- Adjust marketing strategies based on shifts in consumer sentiment.
- Identify emerging trends and concerns that may influence purchasing decisions.

AI models process text, voice, and even facial recognition data to determine sentiment trends. This enables businesses to respond promptly to negative feedback, reinforce positive customer experiences, and refine messaging to align with audience expectations.

AI-Powered Contextual Advertising

Unlike traditional behavioral advertising, which relies on past interactions, AI-powered contextual advertising considers the surrounding digital environment in which an ad is placed. AI evaluates webpage content, user activity, and even situational factors (such as time of day and geographic location) to deliver:

- Highly relevant advertisements tailored to the immediate context of the consumer's browsing session.
- Improved ad placements that align with customer interests without relying solely on historical behavior tracking.

- Compliance-friendly targeting approaches that respect data privacy regulations by avoiding the use of third-party cookies.

This form of advertising provides businesses with a non-intrusive, highly targeted way to engage customers in a meaningful manner.

Predictive Audience Expansion

AI-driven predictive modeling allows businesses to extend their reach beyond existing customer segments by identifying new audiences that share similarities with high-value customers. This process includes:

- Identifying potential customers based on shared behavioral and demographic traits with existing top-performing segments.
- Predicting purchasing intent among untapped audience groups and optimizing marketing strategies accordingly.
- Reducing acquisition costs by focusing on consumers with a higher likelihood of engagement and conversion.

Through predictive audience expansion, companies can enhance their customer acquisition strategies and maximize their return on investment.

AI-driven customer segmentation and targeting enable businesses to refine their marketing efforts by analyzing behavioral patterns, predicting customer intent, and automating audience segmentation. Unlike traditional segmentation methods, AI allows for more granular micro-segmentation, real-time updates, and predictive modeling, helping businesses create highly relevant and personalized marketing strategies.

By leveraging AI-powered tools, businesses can optimize ad targeting, enhance customer engagement, and deliver messaging that aligns with individual preferences. However, successful implementation requires careful data management, seamless integration with existing systems, and compliance with data privacy regulations. Businesses must also strike a balance between automation and human oversight to ensure that AI-driven segmentation remains accurate, ethical, and effective.

Looking ahead, advancements in hyper-personalization, AI-powered sentiment analysis, contextual advertising, and predictive audience expansion will further refine customer targeting strategies. Organizations that embrace these innovations while maintaining transparency and responsible AI usage will be well-positioned to improve marketing efficiency, strengthen customer relationships, and achieve sustainable business growth.

Key Takeaways

- AI enhances segmentation by identifying micro-segments, optimizing ad targeting, personalizing messaging, and automating segmentation updates in real-time.
- Key AI-powered segmentation techniques include demographic, behavioral, psychographic, predictive, and real-time dynamic segmentation.
- Successful AI implementation requires structured data collection, the right segmentation tools, and continuous optimization.
- Challenges such as data quality, system integration, compliance with privacy laws, and over-reliance on automation must be addressed.
- Future trends include AI-powered sentiment analysis, contextual advertising, and predictive audience expansion.

Reflection Questions

- How does your business currently segment customers, and where can AI improve this process?
- What types of AI-driven segmentation techniques could provide better insights into your target audience?
- How can predictive analytics help refine your customer targeting strategies?
- How can you balance AI-driven automation with human oversight to ensure ethical and effective segmentation?

Action Steps

- Assess your current customer segmentation strategy and identify areas where AI could improve targeting and personalization.
- Research AI-powered segmentation tools, such as customer data platforms (CDPs) and AI-driven analytics solutions.
- Enhance your data collection practices to ensure high-quality inputs for AI-driven segmentation models.
- Implement a small-scale test of AI-powered segmentation techniques and track engagement and conversion rates.
- Develop a framework for ongoing AI optimization, ensuring segmentation strategies evolve with customer behaviors and market trends.

PART III
AI FOR CUSTOMER EXPERIENCE AND ENGAGEMENT

MODULE 8
TRANSFORMING CUSTOMER JOURNEYS WITH AUTOMATION

A well-structured customer journey plays a crucial role in ensuring a seamless experience, increasing engagement, and fostering long-term relationships between businesses and their customers. The integration of automation, driven by Artificial Intelligence (AI) and marketing technology (MarTech), has transformed how businesses interact with customers across multiple touchpoints. By leveraging automation, organizations can provide personalized experiences, reduce friction, and improve response times, leading to better customer satisfaction and retention.

This chapter sheds light on how AI-driven automation enhances customer journeys, detailing the key components, implementation strategies, challenges, and emerging trends that will shape the future of automated customer experiences.

UNDERSTANDING CUSTOMER JOURNEY AUTOMATION

Customer journey automation is the use of AI and MarTech to optimize and personalize interactions between businesses and customers throughout the customer lifecycle. By incorporating automation, businesses can:

Streamline the buying process

- Automation helps in segmenting customer journeys, ensuring targeted communication and support.

- It minimizes friction by reducing manual interventions, offering intuitive navigation and simplifying transactions.
- Guided workflows through automated messages ensure customers receive relevant information at each step of their decision-making process.
- Customers receive automated reminders and nudges to complete pending actions, such as unfinished sign-ups or purchases.

Deliver personalized recommendations

- AI-driven recommendation engines analyze customer data, browsing habits, and purchase history to suggest relevant products or services.
- Businesses can tailor marketing efforts to individual customer needs, improving conversion rates and enhancing user experiences.
- Automated personalization allows for dynamic content in emails, website pages, and digital advertisements, ensuring customers see the most relevant offers.
- With machine learning algorithms, recommendations evolve continuously based on real-time user engagement and behavioral changes.

Enhance response times

- AI chatbots and virtual assistants provide instant responses, reducing customer wait times and improving satisfaction levels.
- Automated ticketing systems categorize and prioritize inquiries, ensuring prompt attention to urgent issues.
- AI-driven help desks can retrieve contextual data from previous interactions, enabling quick resolution of recurring customer concerns.

- Businesses can implement automated feedback loops, where customers receive rapid follow-up responses for their queries or complaints.

Reduce manual workloads

- Automation minimizes repetitive administrative tasks such as sending invoices, scheduling follow-ups, and generating reports.
- AI-powered scheduling tools help businesses streamline appointment bookings and customer interactions efficiently.
- Automated data entry and synchronization across multiple platforms eliminate redundancy and reduce human errors.
- Businesses can automate survey collection, feedback analysis, and customer segmentation to refine marketing and sales strategies.

Align marketing, sales, and customer service

- AI-driven automation ensures consistent messaging across different teams, preventing miscommunication or fragmented customer experiences.
- Automated data synchronization between CRM systems, email marketing tools, and customer support platforms creates a unified customer profile.
- Businesses can set up workflow automation to trigger specific actions based on customer behavior, such as sending promotions after a product view.
- Cross-functional automation improves collaboration between departments, allowing real-time updates on customer interactions and preferences.

Automation does not replace human interactions entirely but complements them, ensuring that customers receive timely and relevant information while allowing human teams to focus on more complex queries and strategic decision-making.

KEY AI-POWERED COMPONENTS IN CUSTOMER JOURNEY AUTOMATION

Automated Customer Onboarding

A seamless onboarding experience is critical to customer retention. AI-driven automation simplifies onboarding by:

Sending automated welcome emails:

- Businesses can create structured welcome email sequences introducing new customers to their services or products.
- These emails can include step-by-step tutorials, video demonstrations, or FAQ sections to help users get started.
- AI-driven segmentation allows businesses to personalize welcome emails based on user preferences and behaviors.
- Automated reminders can guide customers through incomplete onboarding steps, ensuring higher engagement rates.

Deploying AI-powered chatbot:

- Chatbots provide 24/7 support by addressing common inquiries, and reducing customer wait times.
- Businesses can integrate chatbots across multiple platforms, including websites, mobile apps, and social media.
- AI-driven chatbots can learn from user interactions, continuously improving responses and providing more relevant information over time.
- Customers can receive real-time troubleshooting support during the onboarding process, minimizing frustration and dropout rates.

Personalizing recommendations:

- AI analyzes customer data to suggest relevant products, services, or learning materials based on past behaviors.
- Personalization engines adapt to customer engagement, refining recommendations as the customer progresses through their journey.
- Businesses can implement dynamic onboarding experiences that adjust based on individual user needs and interests.
- Continuous refinement of customer profiles ensures accuracy in personalized recommendations, leading to better satisfaction and retention.

Behavioral Triggers for Engagement

AI continuously monitors customer interactions and triggers appropriate responses. Key applications include:

Abandoned cart reminders:

- AI identifies when a customer leaves items in their cart and sends follow-up messages encouraging completion.
- Businesses can personalize these reminders with discount offers, product recommendations, or urgency-driven messages.
- Behavioral data helps refine messaging strategies, ensuring effectiveness without overwhelming customers.
- Automated multi-channel reminders (email, SMS, push notifications) improve the likelihood of conversion.

Product recommendations:

- AI tracks browsing behavior and purchase history to generate tailored product suggestions.
- Recommendations can be delivered through various channels, including emails, app notifications, and website banners.
- Businesses can implement real-time recommendations on checkout pages, enhancing cross-selling opportunities.
- AI-driven personalization ensures customers see the most relevant products, improving the likelihood of purchases.

Post-engagement follow-ups:

- AI automation sends personalized messages after a webinar, demo, or content download.
- Follow-ups can include additional resources, special offers, or invitations to related events.
- Businesses can track user engagement with follow-up content and adjust future communications accordingly.
- AI can segment users based on engagement levels, ensuring appropriate follow-up strategies for each group.

Multi-Channel Communication Automation

Customers engage with brands through multiple channels, including email, social media, and live chat. AI helps in:

Coordinating messaging:

- AI ensures consistency in messaging across email, SMS, chatbots, and social media.
- Businesses can automate multi-channel campaigns to maintain customer engagement without manual intervention.
- AI-driven sentiment analysis helps businesses adjust messaging tone based on customer responses.
- Cross-platform data integration provides a unified view of customer interactions, improving communication strategies.

Providing real-time responses:

- AI-powered chatbots and virtual assistants offer instant responses, reducing wait times and improving satisfaction.
- Businesses can implement AI-driven self-service portals to help customers find answers without contacting support teams.
- AI-driven natural language processing (NLP) ensures chatbot interactions remain contextually relevant and human-like.
- Real-time response tracking allows businesses to measure chatbot effectiveness and refine automated support strategies.

Scheduling communications:

- AI automates email and message scheduling, optimizing delivery times for maximum engagement.
- Predictive analytics ensures messages are sent when customers are most likely to respond.
- Businesses can schedule personalized promotional messages, reducing the risk of overloading customers with unnecessary notifications.
- AI-driven automation allows businesses to experiment with different communication strategies through A/B testing.

AI-Driven Lead Nurturing

Businesses must nurture leads effectively to convert them into paying customers. AI enhances lead nurturing by:

Segmenting audiences based on behavior:

- AI analyzes website visits, downloads, and email engagement to segment leads into relevant groups.
- Businesses can personalize marketing efforts based on specific lead behaviors and preferences.
- AI-driven lead scoring identifies high-potential leads, allowing sales teams to focus their efforts effectively.
- Continuous tracking of user behavior ensures accurate audience segmentation over time.

Tracking engagement metrics:

- AI provides insights into customer interactions, including open rates, click-through rates, and content engagement.
- Businesses can adjust nurturing strategies based on real-time engagement data.
- AI helps identify trends in customer behavior, allowing for data-driven decision-making.
- Businesses can integrate AI-driven CRM tools to centralize and analyze customer data more efficiently.

Personalizing outreach efforts:

- AI automates personalized email sequences, ensuring leads receive relevant content at the right time.
- Businesses can create AI-driven drip campaigns that adapt based on user interactions.
- Predictive modeling enables businesses to anticipate customer needs, offering timely solutions.
- AI-generated insights help refine outreach messaging, improving response rates and conversions.

Predictive Customer Support Automation

AI-powered customer support anticipates and addresses customer issues before they escalate. Features include:

Chatbots and virtual assistants:

- AI-driven support bots provide real-time answers to customer inquiries.
- Businesses can integrate chatbots into customer service workflows, reducing agent workload.
- NLP-driven AI enhances chatbot accuracy, improving user experience.
- AI-powered assistants can guide customers through troubleshooting steps efficiently.

Automated ticket routing:

- AI categorizes and assigns customer support tickets based on issue type and urgency.
- Businesses can ensure queries reach the right department, improving resolution times.
- Machine learning models enhance routing accuracy by learning from past interactions.
- Automated triaging ensures priority cases receive immediate attention.

Proactive support:

- AI predicts customer issues based on behavioral data and previous interactions.
- Businesses can initiate proactive engagement, preventing issues from escalating.
- AI-driven alerts notify support teams of potential service disruptions, allowing for rapid response.
- Predictive analytics ensures businesses can offer timely solutions before customers reach out for support.

By integrating AI-driven automation into customer support workflows, businesses can enhance customer satisfaction and streamline service operations, ensuring more efficient problem resolution.

IMPLEMENTING AI-DRIVEN CUSTOMER JOURNEY AUTOMATION

Mapping the Customer Journey

Organizations should define key customer touchpoints and identify areas suitable for automation. The customer journey is typically divided into four stages, each presenting unique opportunities for AI-driven automation:

Awareness Stage:

- AI-powered content recommendations help present the most relevant information to potential customers, increasing brand awareness.
- Automated audience segmentation ensures that targeted digital ads reach the right demographics at optimal times.
- Social listening tools powered by AI track discussions about products and services, enabling businesses to adjust messaging and engagement strategies.

- AI-driven chatbots on websites or social media engage visitors, answering queries and directing them to appropriate resources.

Consideration Stage:

- Automated email sequences nurture leads by sending informative content, case studies, and product comparisons to help customers make informed decisions.
- Retargeting ads powered by AI help remind customers about products or services they previously explored but have not yet purchased.
- AI-based recommendation engines suggest similar or complementary products based on customer browsing behaviors, increasing the likelihood of conversion.
- Virtual assistants guide potential buyers through FAQs, ensuring they receive relevant information without human intervention.

Purchase Stage:

- AI-enhanced checkout experiences streamline the buying process, reducing cart abandonment through automated reminders and personalized discounts.
- Dynamic pricing algorithms adjust prices based on demand, customer behavior, and market trends, optimizing sales strategies.
- AI-powered fraud detection identifies potential risks in transactions, improving security and ensuring a seamless purchase experience.
- Automated confirmation emails and real-time order tracking updates enhance customer confidence and satisfaction.

Retention Stage:

- AI-driven loyalty programs analyze customer behavior and offer personalized rewards, increasing repeat purchases and long-term engagement.

- Automated post-purchase engagement strategies, such as follow-up emails with usage tips or satisfaction surveys, strengthen customer relationships.
- AI-powered customer support chatbots provide instant responses to queries, ensuring continued engagement after the sale.
- Predictive analytics identify customers who may be at risk of churning, triggering targeted retention strategies.

Selecting the Right Automation Tools

Businesses can choose from various AI-powered automation tools to streamline customer journey management. Some key categories include:

Customer Data Platforms (CDPs):

- Consolidate data from multiple sources, creating a unified customer profile that enhances personalization.
- Use AI algorithms to analyze customer interactions, providing actionable insights for marketing and sales teams.
- Improve segmentation and targeting efforts by leveraging predictive analytics to anticipate customer behavior.

Marketing Automation Software:

- Automate email marketing campaigns, ensuring timely and relevant communication with leads and customers.
- Implement AI-driven triggers to send messages based on customer interactions, such as website visits, downloads, or abandoned carts.
- Enable multi-channel automation, coordinating email, social media, and SMS campaigns for a cohesive marketing strategy.

AI Chatbots:

- Provide real-time customer service by handling inquiries, processing orders, and directing users to the appropriate resources.
- Learn from past interactions to refine responses and improve user experiences over time.
- Integrate with CRM systems, ensuring personalized support and seamless transitions between automated and human-assisted interactions.

Personalizing Customer Interactions

AI-driven automation allows for highly personalized interactions tailored to individual customer behaviors and preferences. Key applications include:

Dynamic Content Customization:

- AI analyzes user behavior to deliver personalized website content, adjusting banners, product recommendations, and landing pages in real-time.
- Automated content delivery ensures users receive relevant blog posts, videos, or tutorials based on their browsing history.
- Email campaigns utilize AI-generated content variations, ensuring that messages resonate with different audience segments.

Adaptive Email Sequences:

- AI-powered workflows adjust email sequences based on how customers engage with previous messages.
- Segmentation ensures users receive customized messages based on their actions, such as clicking a link, downloading an eBook, or making a purchase.
- Predictive analytics help determine the optimal timing and frequency of email outreach, reducing unsubscribes and improving open rates.

Predictive Analytics:

- AI anticipates customer needs by analyzing data from past interactions, allowing businesses to proactively offer relevant solutions.
- Customer sentiment analysis helps identify satisfaction levels, enabling companies to tailor responses and engagement efforts accordingly.
- Predictive modeling assists in forecasting demand, helping businesses adjust inventory and marketing strategies to align with customer expectations.

Monitoring and Optimizing Automated Workflows

To maximize the effectiveness of AI-driven automation, businesses must continuously monitor and refine their workflows. Important strategies include:

Analyze Performance Metrics:

- Track engagement rates, conversion rates, and customer satisfaction scores to measure the impact of automation.
- AI-powered analytics tools provide detailed reports on campaign effectiveness, highlighting areas for improvement.
- Heatmaps and user tracking tools offer insights into how customers interact with automated touchpoints.

Adjust AI-Driven Workflows:

- Automation systems should be regularly updated based on performance data and customer feedback.
- AI models can be retrained to improve accuracy and relevance in content recommendations, chatbot interactions, and automated messaging.
- Businesses should conduct periodic reviews of automated workflows to ensure they align with evolving customer expectations.

Conduct A/B Testing:

- Split testing different versions of automated messages, landing pages, and recommendation algorithms helps identify what resonates best with customers.
- AI-driven testing tools automate A/B experiments, continuously optimizing messaging, timing, and targeting.
- Insights from A/B tests inform data-driven decision-making, ensuring automation strategies evolve with customer behavior trends.

By integrating these AI-driven automation strategies, businesses can create seamless, personalized, and efficient customer journeys that enhance engagement and retention while optimizing internal processes.

CHALLENGES IN AI-DRIVEN CUSTOMER JOURNEY AUTOMATION

Data Integration and Quality

Accurate data is crucial for AI automation. Organizations must:

Ensure seamless data integration across CRM, email, and customer support systems. This requires businesses to use standardized data formats, establish robust APIs, and leverage middleware solutions to facilitate smooth data flow between different platforms. Without seamless integration, data silos can form, making it challenging to achieve a unified view of customer interactions.

Maintain data hygiene by eliminating duplicate, outdated, or inaccurate information. Poor data quality can result in misleading insights and ineffective AI-driven automation. Businesses should regularly audit their databases, implement validation protocols, and utilize AI-powered data cleansing tools to ensure accuracy and consistency across customer records. Investing in automated data governance solutions can also help organizations enforce policies that maintain data integrity over time.

Balancing Automation with Human Interaction

Despite AI advancements, human oversight is necessary for:

Handling complex customer issues that require empathy and detailed responses. AI can effectively manage routine queries, but more nuanced issues, such as emotionally charged complaints or highly specific troubleshooting, still benefit from human intervention. To strike the right balance, businesses should deploy AI as a first-line responder while maintaining an escalation pathway for human agents to step in when needed.

Ensuring chatbot interactions remain natural and contextually relevant. AI-driven chatbots must be continuously trained to understand context, recognize customer sentiment, and avoid repetitive or irrelevant responses. Incorporating natural language processing (NLP) improvements, sentiment analysis, and periodic human oversight ensures that AI remains an effective communication tool without alienating customers through mechanical or impersonal interactions.

Customer Privacy and Compliance

Businesses must adhere to data protection laws like GDPR and CCPA by:

Being transparent about AI-driven processes. Customers have a right to understand how their data is being used, especially when AI is involved. Businesses should clearly communicate their data collection, processing, and storage practices in their privacy policies. AI-generated decisions should be explainable, ensuring customers feel confident in their interactions with automated systems.

Providing customers with control over their data and preferences. Offering customers the ability to manage their privacy settings, opt out of AI-driven personalization, or request data deletion helps businesses build trust. Implementing robust consent management tools and ensuring compliance with privacy regulations not only protects users but also enhances brand reputation. AI automation should be designed with privacy by default, ensuring that only the necessary data is used for each interaction.

Ensuring AI Accuracy and Context Awareness

Continuous monitoring helps:

Avoid irrelevant recommendations. AI-driven automation relies on data patterns to generate personalized content and suggestions. However, inaccurate or outdated data can lead to irrelevant recommendations that frustrate customers. To improve accuracy, businesses should regularly update AI models, incorporate real-time feedback loops, and refine their recommendation algorithms based on evolving customer preferences.

Refine predictive models for better customer engagement. Predictive analytics can enhance customer experience by anticipating needs, but these models must be continuously validated to ensure reliability. Businesses should employ AI performance tracking, conduct A/B testing on automated recommendations, and incorporate customer feedback to fine-tune AI-driven interactions. By integrating contextual awareness into AI decision-making, businesses can create a more adaptive and responsive customer journey automation system.

FUTURE TRENDS IN AI-DRIVEN CUSTOMER JOURNEY AUTOMATION

Hyper-Personalized AI Experiences

Real-time personalization based on contextual data. AI-driven personalization involves analyzing user interactions, preferences, and behaviors in real time. Businesses leverage AI algorithms to dynamically adjust website layouts, product recommendations, and email content based on customer profiles. By continuously refining personalization models, organizations can enhance customer satisfaction and engagement. This level of personalization requires robust data collection, ethical handling of user information, and AI models that evolve with customer interactions.

Dynamic website and email content tailored to individual preferences. AI systems enable businesses to create personalized content that aligns with user preferences. Websites can display different homepage versions based on browsing history, while email marketing campaigns can feature unique offers based on previous interactions. This approach increases the likelihood of customer engagement and conversion, but it also demands a well-structured data strategy to ensure accuracy and relevance in content recommendations.

Conversational AI and Voice Assistants

Enhanced voice search and virtual assistant interactions. As more consumers adopt voice-enabled devices, businesses must optimize for voice-based interactions. AI-powered voice assistants can provide instant responses, streamline navigation, and offer personalized recommendations based on past interactions. This requires an understanding of natural language processing (NLP) and continuous refinement of AI models to improve accuracy and user experience.

Chatbots that handle voice and text-based queries seamlessly. Conversational AI enhances customer service by offering real-time assistance across multiple communication channels. Chatbots equipped with advanced NLP can comprehend customer queries, process context, and deliver relevant responses. Additionally, integrating chatbots with CRM systems ensures that interactions remain consistent, improving overall user experience. Businesses implementing these solutions must focus on designing intuitive workflows that prioritize user needs and minimize frustration.

AI-Powered Predictive Customer Journeys

Anticipating customer needs before they arise. AI models analyze behavioral patterns and historical data to predict customer intent. Businesses can utilize predictive analytics to identify when customers are likely to make a purchase, seek support, or disengage. By proactively addressing potential concerns or offering relevant recommendations, organizations can enhance customer retention and satisfaction. However, predictive modeling requires accurate data and ongoing optimization to remain effective and relevant.

Automating proactive engagement strategies for improved retention. AI-powered automation enables businesses to initiate engagement based on customer behavior. Automated email reminders, personalized offers, and AI-driven notifications help maintain customer interest. Predictive models also assist in identifying customers who may churn, allowing businesses to implement targeted retention strategies. To maximize effectiveness, companies must continuously evaluate and refine these engagement mechanisms based on customer feedback and data insights.

Seamless Cross-Channel Automation

Unifying data across platforms for a cohesive experience. Businesses operate across multiple digital channels, including websites, mobile apps, social media, and email. AI-driven automation ensures that customer interactions remain consistent across these touchpoints. By centralizing customer data, organizations can provide a more seamless experience, reducing friction in the customer journey. Achieving this requires integration between various AI tools, CRM systems, and marketing platforms to synchronize data and improve personalization.

Automating interactions across multiple digital channels. AI-driven automation streamlines customer interactions by managing communications across different platforms. Automated workflows ensure that users receive relevant information regardless of the channel they engage with. Whether through AI-powered chatbots, automated email sequences, or personalized social media engagement, businesses can create a cohesive experience. To succeed, companies need to monitor engagement metrics and adjust AI-driven strategies based on user feedback and changing preferences.

AI-driven automation plays an important role in enhancing customer journeys by streamlining interactions, improving engagement, and optimizing marketing and support processes. By integrating AI into customer journey automation, businesses can deliver personalized experiences, respond to customer needs more efficiently, and ensure consistency across multiple touchpoints.

Automation improves efficiency by reducing manual workloads, allowing businesses to focus on strategic initiatives while AI-driven tools manage routine interactions. From onboarding and engagement to support and retention, AI helps businesses anticipate customer needs and deliver relevant responses in real time. However, successful implementation requires careful planning, high-quality data management, and ongoing optimization to ensure that AI-driven interactions remain accurate and meaningful.

Balancing automation with human oversight remains essential to maintaining authenticity in customer interactions. While AI enhances efficiency, human involvement ensures that complex issues are handled with empathy and contextual understanding. Additionally, businesses must navigate challenges related to data integration, privacy compliance, and AI accuracy to maintain customer trust and regulatory adherence.

Looking ahead, advancements in hyper-personalization, predictive analytics, conversational AI, and cross-channel automation will further refine customer journey strategies. Businesses that adopt AI thoughtfully, continuously optimize their workflows, and prioritize customer experience will be better positioned to build stronger relationships and drive sustainable engagement.

Key Takeaways

- Customer journey automation leverages AI and marketing technology (MarTech) to streamline interactions, enhance personalization, and optimize response times.
- AI-powered onboarding improves customer retention through automated welcome emails, chatbots, and personalized recommendations.
- Behavioral triggers such as abandoned cart reminders, product recommendations, and post-engagement follow-ups increase engagement and conversions.
- Multi-channel automation ensures seamless communication across email, social media, and chatbots, enhancing customer experience.
- AI-driven lead nurturing uses segmentation, engagement tracking, and predictive analytics to personalize outreach and improve conversions.

Reflection Questions

- What specific pain points do your customers experience that AI-driven automation could help address?
- How can you balance automation with human interaction to ensure a seamless and personalized customer experience?
- How can predictive analytics enhance your engagement strategies and improve customer retention?

Action Steps

- Map out your customer touchpoints and identify areas where automation can improve efficiency and personalization.
- Evaluate AI-driven automation solutions such as chatbots, CRM integrations, and recommendation engines to enhance customer interactions.
- Set up automated reminders, follow-ups, and recommendations based on customer interactions.
- Regularly review engagement metrics, conversion rates, and customer feedback to optimize automation workflows.
- Establish data governance protocols to maintain transparency, accuracy, and compliance with privacy regulations.

MODULE 9
AI-ENABLED CONTENT CREATION AND OPTIMIZATION

Content creation is an essential aspect of digital marketing, significantly impacting brand perception, customer engagement, and conversion rates. The integration of artificial intelligence (AI) into content marketing has transformed how businesses generate, distribute, and optimize content. AI-powered tools assist in writing, editing, analyzing, and distributing content more efficiently, helping businesses streamline workflows and enhance their marketing strategies. This chapter explores how AI contributes to content creation, optimization strategies, implementation best practices, challenges, and future trends.

THE ROLE OF AI IN CONTENT CREATION

AI enhances content marketing by automating repetitive tasks and providing data-driven insights to optimize content strategies. With the rapid development of machine learning models and natural language processing (NLP), AI can generate human-like text, suggest improvements, and predict content performance based on analytics. Some key AI-powered capabilities include:

Natural Language Processing (NLP)

Natural Language Processing (NLP) enables AI to interpret, generate, and refine human language, playing a crucial role in content marketing. NLP algorithms analyze text to detect tone, structure, grammar, and intent, allowing AI to generate coherent and contextually relevant content. Businesses use NLP-driven tools to improve readability, refine messaging, and generate automated reports or summaries. NLP-powered chatbots enhance customer service by responding dynamically to inquiries based on contextual understanding. Additionally, sentiment analysis tools driven by NLP help businesses gauge audience reactions, refining messaging strategies accordingly.

Automated Content Generation

AI-driven automated content generation simplifies the content creation process for businesses. AI tools can produce drafts of blog posts, product descriptions, and social media updates based on predefined keywords, industry trends, and target audience preferences. AI-powered writing assistants suggest alternative phrasing, reword complex sentences, and offer grammatical corrections. By integrating structured data, AI enhances content relevance, making it more informative and engaging for readers. Businesses utilize AI-generated content as a foundation for further refinement by human editors, ensuring quality and originality while optimizing production efficiency.

SEO Optimization

Search Engine Optimization (SEO) remains a critical aspect of digital content strategy, and AI significantly enhances optimization efforts. AI tools analyze vast datasets to identify trending keywords, predict search intent, and suggest improvements for meta descriptions, headers, and readability. AI-driven SEO software examines search rankings in real time, providing recommendations to enhance visibility. Businesses utilize AI to optimize on-page SEO elements, improve backlink strategies, and ensure that content aligns with evolving search algorithms. Additionally, AI assesses competitors' content performance, helping brands refine their strategies to achieve higher organic rankings.

Content Personalization

AI enables businesses to personalize content based on user behavior, preferences, and demographic data. AI-driven personalization tools analyze browsing patterns, purchase history, and engagement levels to tailor content recommendations for individual users. Dynamic content personalization enhances user experience by delivering relevant messages at the right time. Businesses employ AI to segment audiences, customize email marketing campaigns, and recommend personalized blog articles or product suggestions. AI-powered recommendation engines, such as those used by streaming platforms and e-commerce websites, refine content offerings based on historical interactions, ensuring an engaging and individualized user experience.

Performance Analysis

AI-driven analytics tools evaluate content performance by analyzing engagement metrics such as click-through rates, bounce rates, and social shares. These insights help businesses refine their content strategies for better audience engagement. AI-powered dashboards track content effectiveness in real time, offering actionable recommendations to enhance user interaction. Businesses leverage AI to conduct A/B testing on different content variations, identifying the most effective messaging and visual elements. AI-driven analytics also assess audience sentiment, providing deeper insights into content reception and areas for improvement. With AI-enhanced performance tracking, businesses can make data-driven decisions to optimize their content marketing strategies continuously.

AI-POWERED CONTENT CREATION TOOLS

AI tools have become increasingly sophisticated, providing support across multiple content formats and channels. Some widely used AI-driven platforms include:

GPT-based Writing Assistants

AI-powered writing assistants use natural language processing models to generate text based on prompts and keywords. These tools help content creators by producing structured, contextually relevant drafts. Businesses leverage these tools for writing blog posts, product descriptions, email campaigns, and even technical documentation. Writing assistants also help improve grammar, sentence structure, and readability, making the content more accessible and engaging for readers. Additionally, AI-powered editors offer suggestions for tone adjustments and clarity improvements, enabling users to refine messaging for different audience segments.

AI Image and Video Generators

AI-driven tools can generate high-quality visual content, including images, infographics, and videos. These platforms use machine learning algorithms to create visuals that align with brand aesthetics and marketing goals. AI video generators automate tasks such as scriptwriting, scene generation, and editing. Some tools even provide real-time translation and transcription features, making content more accessible across diverse linguistic and geographic audiences. Brands use AI-generated images and videos in advertisements, social media posts, and educational content, ensuring consistency and efficiency in visual storytelling.

SEO Optimization Software

AI-powered SEO tools help content marketers enhance search engine rankings by providing data-driven insights. These platforms analyze search trends, identify relevant keywords, and offer suggestions for optimizing metadata, headings, and readability. AI-driven SEO software also evaluates website performance, providing actionable recommendations to improve load times, keyword density, and internal linking structures. With AI-powered content audits, marketers can refine existing content, ensuring that it aligns with evolving search engine algorithms and user expectations. Businesses use these insights to develop a more strategic approach to content planning and distribution.

Chatbots for Conversational Content

Chatbots powered by AI enable businesses to interact with users dynamically through automated messaging systems. These bots provide instant responses to customer queries, enhancing engagement and improving user experience. AI-driven chatbots are widely used in customer support, lead generation, and e-commerce applications. By processing natural language inputs, chatbots provide personalized recommendations, troubleshoot common issues, and assist users in navigating digital platforms. Businesses benefit from AI-powered chatbots by reducing response times, improving customer satisfaction, and automating repetitive interactions, allowing human agents to focus on more complex tasks.

APPLICATIONS OF AI IN CONTENT CREATION

Automated Article and Blog Writing

AI assists in content writing by:

- Generating drafts based on specific keywords and themes, allowing writers to quickly develop content that aligns with industry trends and audience interests.
- Suggesting engaging headlines by analyzing past performance data, ensuring titles capture user attention while maintaining relevance to the subject matter.
- Structuring articles for readability by identifying logical flow, breaking up large text blocks, and recommending appropriate formatting elements such as bullet points and subheadings.

- Summarizing long-form content into key points, making information more digestible for readers who prefer quick insights over extensive reading.
- Assisting in research by pulling relevant data and citations from trusted sources, enhancing content credibility and accuracy.

AI-Powered Content Curation

AI curates content by analyzing user preferences and recommending relevant articles, videos, or social media posts. This enables marketers to:

- Deliver personalized content feeds by understanding user behavior, past interactions, and demographic data, ensuring audiences receive material tailored to their interests.
- Maintain audience engagement through continuous updates by tracking trending topics, industry developments, and real-time conversations, helping brands stay relevant in evolving digital landscapes.
- Optimize content calendars by suggesting the most effective times for publishing based on user engagement trends, maximizing visibility and impact.
- Filter through large volumes of content and identify high-quality pieces, reducing the effort required for manual curation and improving the consistency of shared materials.
- Recommend multimedia content formats based on audience consumption patterns, ensuring users receive a mix of text, video, and interactive elements.

Social Media Content Generation

AI automates social media content creation by:

- Crafting compelling captions and hashtags using sentiment analysis and engagement data, ensuring posts resonate with target audiences.

- Scheduling posts for optimal reach by analyzing historical engagement patterns, maximizing audience interaction during peak activity hours.
- Analyzing user interactions to refine content strategies, helping brands adjust their messaging based on audience responses and feedback.
- Monitoring competitors' social media activities and suggesting improvements in content style, frequency, and engagement techniques.
- Generating automated responses for customer inquiries, improving responsiveness while maintaining a consistent brand voice.
- Creating A/B testing scenarios to compare different post styles and formats, allowing marketers to identify the most effective approaches for engagement and reach.

SEO Content Optimization

AI-driven SEO tools analyze search intent and suggest enhancements for better ranking. These tools help marketers:

- Identify high-performing keywords by assessing competition levels, search volume, and user intent, refining content strategies for better organic reach.
- Improve content readability by analyzing sentence structure, complexity, and clarity, ensuring articles are accessible to a wider audience.
- Optimize page elements such as titles, headers, and meta descriptions by incorporating AI-generated recommendations tailored to current search engine algorithms.
- Generate alternative phrasing suggestions to improve search engine rankings without compromising readability or user experience.
- Analyze backlink opportunities by identifying reputable sources, helping businesses strengthen their domain authority.

- Track real-time SEO performance metrics and adjust strategies accordingly, ensuring continuous improvement and alignment with evolving ranking criteria.

AI-Powered Video and Visual Content Creation

AI-generated visuals, including infographics, animations, and video content, support digital marketing strategies. AI tools enable:

- Automated video editing by detecting highlights, suggesting relevant transitions, and optimizing audio synchronization, streamlining production processes.
- Personalized visual recommendations based on audience preferences, enhancing engagement by delivering visuals tailored to specific user interests.
- Real-time enhancements such as object recognition, background adjustments, and facial expression analysis, improving video production quality and consistency.
- Captioning and subtitle generation for accessibility, expanding content reach to users with hearing impairments or those consuming content in noisy environments.
- Conversion of long-form text content into visual summaries, helping brands repurpose written material into more engaging and shareable formats.
- AI-driven image recognition technology that identifies the most effective visual elements for increasing engagement, improving post-performance on social media and marketing campaigns.

IMPLEMENTING AI IN CONTENT OPTIMIZATION

Aligning AI Content Strategies with Business Goals

Before integrating AI-driven content tools, businesses should define their objectives. A well-structured AI content strategy ensures that marketing efforts align with organizational goals and effectively meet audience expectations. Common objectives include:

Increasing Brand Awareness | AI-powered tools analyze market trends and competitor strategies to create content that enhances visibility and resonates with target audiences.

Enhancing Audience Engagement | AI tools personalize content distribution based on user preferences, ensuring that the right message reaches the right audience at the right time.

Improving Conversion Rates | AI-driven insights allow businesses to refine messaging and target potential customers more effectively, increasing the likelihood of conversions and sales.

By establishing clear goals, businesses can integrate AI tools strategically, ensuring that content initiatives contribute to long-term growth and customer retention.

Choosing the Right AI Content Tools

Selecting AI-powered platforms based on content needs ensures effective implementation. Businesses should evaluate AI tools using the following criteria:

Integration Capabilities | AI solutions should seamlessly integrate with existing content management systems (CMS), marketing automation tools, and customer relationship management (CRM) software.

- **Usability and Learning Curve** | AI tools should be user-friendly, enabling content creators to leverage automation without requiring extensive technical expertise.
- **Performance Analytics Features** | Businesses should select AI tools that offer real-time performance tracking, audience behavior analysis, and content optimization recommendations.
- **Customization Options** | AI-driven tools should allow businesses to tailor content based on industry-specific needs and unique brand requirements.

A thorough evaluation process ensures that AI solutions enhance content workflows and align with broader marketing strategies.

Enhancing Human-AI Collaboration

AI should complement human creativity rather than replace it. Effective collaboration between AI tools and human content creators ensures that content maintains authenticity, emotional depth, and brand consistency. Best practices include:

Using AI-Generated Drafts as a Starting Point | Content creators can leverage AI-generated drafts to accelerate the writing process, then refine the content to enhance its uniqueness and brand voice.

Leveraging AI for Tone and Clarity Optimization | AI-powered tools provide suggestions to improve sentence structure, readability, and coherence while ensuring consistency in tone and messaging.

Ensuring Brand Authenticity | AI-generated content should be reviewed and customized to align with the company's identity, avoiding overly generic or robotic messaging.

Encouraging Cross-Team Collaboration | Marketing teams should work alongside AI tools to align content strategies with broader business objectives, ensuring that automation enhances rather than dictates creative direction.

By balancing automation with human oversight, businesses can maximize efficiency while preserving creativity and originality in their content.

Testing and Measuring Content Performance

Continuous optimization is key to content success. Businesses should establish performance measurement frameworks that assess AI-generated content effectiveness and guide future improvements. Key steps include:

Conducting A/B Testing | AI tools can generate multiple variations of headlines, meta descriptions, and call-to-action (CTA) messages. A/B testing allows marketers to determine which versions resonate most with audiences.

Monitoring Key Performance Indicators (KPIs | Businesses should track engagement metrics such as click-through rates (CTR), bounce rates, time on page, and social media shares to evaluate content effectiveness.

Analyzing User Feedback | AI-powered sentiment analysis tools can assess audience reactions, providing insights into how content is perceived and identifying areas for refinement.

Adjusting Content Strategies Based on Data | AI-driven insights enable marketers to refine content distribution, tailor messaging, and improve targeting strategies in real time.

By consistently evaluating AI-generated content performance, businesses can refine their content strategies, ensuring that AI-driven initiatives contribute to overall marketing success.

CHALLENGES IN AI-ENABLED CONTENT CREATION AND OPTIMIZATION

Ensuring Content Originality and Authenticity

AI-generated content may lack originality and emotional depth, which can affect its ability to resonate with audiences. Marketers should consider the following approaches to maintain authenticity and originality:

Human-Led Editing and Review | AI-generated content should serve as a starting point rather than a finished product. Content teams should refine AI-produced material by adding unique insights, industry-specific knowledge, and brand personality.

Fact-Checking and Source Validation | AI models rely on existing data sources, which may not always be accurate or up to date. Marketers must cross-check facts, statistics, and claims to ensure credibility before publishing.

Brand Voice and Consistency | AI-generated text may sometimes lack the tone, nuance, or style unique to a brand. Reviewing content for consistency in messaging and tone helps maintain a unified brand voice across all platforms.

Combining AI Efficiency with Human Creativity | While AI can generate drafts quickly, human creativity ensures that content includes fresh perspectives, storytelling elements, and emotional appeal, making it more engaging for readers.

Avoiding Redundancy and Plagiarism | AI-generated content should be run through plagiarism detection tools to ensure it does not duplicate existing material. Marketers can also enhance originality by integrating proprietary research, expert opinions, or first-hand case studies.

Balancing Automation and Creativity

AI speeds up content production, but human creativity remains essential for storytelling, emotional connection, and brand differentiation. To strike a balance between automation and creative originality, businesses should:

Use AI for Efficiency, Not Replacement | AI can handle repetitive tasks such as content structuring, keyword optimization, and summarization. However, the final refinement, creative ideation, and storytelling should be left to human marketers and writers.

Incorporate Personalization with Human Insights | AI can personalize content based on user behavior, but human input ensures that personalization is done with empathy and cultural awareness.

Maintain a Flexible Content Strategy | AI models evolve over time, and creative teams should remain adaptable, experimenting with different formats, narratives, and styles while integrating AI assistance.

Enhance Storytelling through AI Insights | AI-driven analytics provide valuable insights into audience behavior. Marketers can use these insights to refine their storytelling approach, ensuring content resonates with users while maintaining authenticity.

Experiment with Hybrid Content Creation Models | Many brands are now blending AI-generated content with human input. For example, AI may generate initial drafts, while human writers refine the message, ensuring it aligns with company goals and audience expectations.

Data Privacy and Ethical Considerations

AI relies on user data for content personalization, which raises privacy and ethical concerns. Businesses must ensure compliance with data protection laws and maintain transparency in AI-driven content strategies. Key considerations include:

Regulatory Compliance | Organizations must adhere to data protection regulations. This includes obtaining user consent before collecting or using personal data.

User Anonymity and Data Security | AI systems should be designed to protect user data by anonymizing personally identifiable information (PII) and employing strong encryption techniques.

Transparency in AI Content Creation | Businesses should disclose when AI is used to generate content, ensuring users are aware of the role of automation in content delivery.

Bias Mitigation in AI Models | AI-generated content can sometimes reflect biases present in training data. Companies should regularly audit AI models for potential biases and implement corrective measures to ensure fairness in content representation.

Ethical AI Use in Content Marketing | Organizations should establish ethical guidelines for AI-generated content, ensuring that AI tools are used responsibly and do not contribute to misinformation or deceptive practices.

Adapting to Evolving AI Capabilities

AI models improve over time, requiring businesses to continuously evaluate AI tools and upgrade their content strategies. To stay ahead of AI advancements, organizations should:

Monitor AI Developments | Keeping up with emerging AI technologies allows businesses to leverage new features and improvements for more effective content strategies.

Evaluate AI Performance Regularly | AI tools should be assessed periodically to determine their impact on content quality, SEO rankings, and audience engagement. Adjustments should be made as needed to optimize AI integration.

Train Teams on AI Utilization | AI adoption should be complemented by employee training programs to ensure marketing teams understand how to use AI tools effectively while maintaining quality control.

Incorporate Feedback Loops | Businesses should collect feedback from audiences and internal teams regarding AI-generated content. This helps refine AI applications and improve content relevance and effectiveness.

Remain Adaptable to AI Evolution | AI is a rapidly evolving field, and businesses must remain agile in adopting new AI-driven content strategies while ensuring alignment with brand goals and industry trends.

By implementing these approaches, businesses can effectively balance AI automation with human creativity, ensuring that content remains original, ethical, and engaging while leveraging the benefits of AI-powered efficiencies.

FUTURE TRENDS IN AI-DRIVEN CONTENT CREATION AND OPTIMIZATION

Advanced Personalization with AI

AI will continue to refine real-time personalization strategies, transforming how businesses engage with their audiences. This involves:

Adapting Content Dynamically | AI analyzes user engagement patterns, such as browsing behavior, click-through rates, and time spent on content, to modify and tailor messaging dynamically. By understanding these patterns, AI-driven systems can present users with content that aligns with their interests and past interactions.

Enhancing Recommendation Systems | AI-generated recommendations leverage historical data and predictive analytics to improve targeted messaging. Content can be adapted based on demographics, user behavior, or even external factors such as location and seasonality. Businesses use AI to suggest relevant blog posts, personalized email campaigns, and curated social media updates to foster stronger connections with their audience.

Utilizing Predictive Analytics | AI can anticipate user needs by analyzing past behavior and predicting future interests. For example, e-commerce platforms can recommend products based on browsing history, while streaming services can suggest shows based on viewing habits. This level of personalization helps businesses create more meaningful interactions with their customers.

Refining Customer Segmentation | AI enables more precise audience segmentation by identifying micro-segments based on user preferences. Traditional marketing strategies rely on broad customer categories, but AI refines these groups based on real-time data, making messaging more relevant and impactful.

AI-Generated Interactive Content

Future AI tools will focus on creating more immersive and engaging experiences through interactive content. This shift includes:

Automated Quizzes and Assessments | AI will design quizzes and assessments that adapt in real-time based on user responses. Businesses can use this for lead generation, customer engagement, and personalized recommendations. For example, e-learning platforms can customize assessments based on student performance, while e-commerce sites can suggest products based on quiz responses.

AI-Generated Augmented Reality (AR) and Virtual Reality (VR) Content | AI will play a crucial role in enhancing AR and VR experiences. This includes generating interactive product visualizations, virtual showrooms, and immersive training simulations. AI can also assist in adapting these experiences based on user interactions, making them more personalized and effective.

Gamification and Adaptive Learning Experiences | AI can dynamically adjust gamified experiences based on user performance. Whether in education, entertainment, or marketing, AI can tailor game mechanics, difficulty levels, and rewards to keep users engaged and motivated.

AI-Enhanced Storytelling in Interactive Media | AI can generate and modify narratives based on user choices in interactive storytelling. This is particularly useful in gaming, marketing campaigns, and virtual simulations, where user input influences story progression.

Voice and Conversational AI for Content Marketing

As voice search and conversational AI continue to expand,

businesses must optimize content for voice-based interactions. Key trends include:

Enhancing Voice-Assisted Shopping and Digital Interactions | AI-driven voice assistants are increasingly used for online shopping, customer support, and content discovery. Brands will need to create voice-friendly content that aligns with natural language queries.

Optimizing for AI-Powered Digital Assistants | Digital assistants like Alexa, Google Assistant, and Siri are becoming primary search tools. Businesses should ensure their content is structured for voice search optimization by incorporating natural language queries, concise answers, and question-based formats.

Improving Conversational AI Chatbots | AI chatbots will continue to evolve, providing more nuanced and human-like interactions. Advanced NLP algorithms will enable chatbots to understand context better, respond with greater accuracy, and offer personalized recommendations based on past conversations.

Expanding Multi-Language and Regional Optimization | As AI becomes more sophisticated, businesses can create multilingual content that adapts to regional dialects and cultural nuances, making global content strategies more effective.

AI-Driven Video Content Enhancement

AI will further advance video content strategies by making production and distribution more efficient and personalized. This evolution will involve:

Automating Scriptwriting and Video Editing Processes | AI-powered tools will assist in scriptwriting by analyzing trending topics, audience preferences, and past engagement data. Video editing tools will automate transitions, captioning, and scene selection, allowing creators to focus on storytelling rather than technical aspects.

Personalizing Video Recommendations for Different Audience Segments | AI will improve content recommendation algorithms to provide highly relevant video suggestions. Streaming services, social media platforms, and e-learning sites will benefit from AI-driven content curation.

Enhancing Real-Time Video Transcription and Translation | AI-powered tools will provide real-time captions and translations, making video content more accessible to a broader audience. Businesses can reach global markets by offering language-optimized video content with minimal manual effort.

Integrating AI-Powered Video Search and Tagging | AI will enable more precise video searches by automatically tagging and categorizing video content based on objects, speech, and user engagement data. This will improve discoverability and search engine rankings for video content.

Applying AI for Real-Time Video Customization | AI will allow businesses to dynamically adjust video content based on user preferences, such as personalized advertisements, interactive overlays, and adaptive storytelling elements.

AI has become an integral part of content creation and optimization, helping businesses streamline workflows, enhance personalization, and improve content performance. Through automation, AI assists in generating written, visual, and interactive content while providing valuable insights for refining marketing strategies. Businesses can leverage AI to improve efficiency, enhance audience engagement, and maintain a data-driven approach to content distribution.

Despite its benefits, AI-generated content still requires human oversight to ensure originality, authenticity, and alignment with brand messaging. Businesses must strike a balance between automation and creativity, using AI as a tool to support, rather than replace, human-driven storytelling and strategic planning.

As AI technology continues to evolve, its capabilities in content marketing will expand. Future advancements in predictive analytics, interactive content, conversational AI, and video personalization will further refine how businesses create and distribute content. Organizations that adopt AI-driven content strategies thoughtfully, while maintaining a focus on quality and ethical considerations, will be well-positioned to adapt to the changing digital landscape and meet the expectations of their audiences.

Key Takeaways

- AI enhances content creation by automating tasks such as writing, editing, and SEO optimization, enabling businesses to improve efficiency and engagement.
- Natural Language Processing (NLP) helps refine content by analyzing tone, grammar, and audience sentiment.
- AI-generated content can serve as a foundation for human editors to ensure quality, originality, and brand alignment.
- AI-driven personalization tailors content based on user preferences, improving engagement and conversion rates.
- AI-powered analytics provide actionable insights, enabling businesses to optimize content strategies based on performance data.

Reflection Questions

- How can AI tools improve your current content creation and marketing efforts?
- Which aspects of your content strategy would benefit the most from automation?
- What measures can you take to ensure AI-generated content aligns with your brand's voice and authenticity?
- How do you balance AI's efficiency with human creativity in your content development process?
- Are there ethical or privacy concerns you need to address when integrating AI into your content strategy?

Action Steps

- Identify areas in your content workflow where AI can enhance productivity and efficiency.
- Test AI-powered tools for content generation, editing, and SEO optimization to understand their capabilities.
- Implement AI-driven analytics to measure content performance and adjust strategies accordingly.
- Develop guidelines to maintain brand authenticity when using AI-generated content.
- Stay informed about evolving AI trends and best practices in content marketing to remain competitive.

PART IV
AI IN MARKETING CHANNELS AND PERFORMANCE OPTIMIZATION

MODULE 10 CONVERSATIONAL AI AND CHATBOTS FOR CUSTOMER ENGAGEMENT

After the rise of AI-powered chatbots, conversational AI and chatbots have become integral tools for customer engagement, helping businesses streamline communication, provide real-time support, and enhance customer experiences. These AI-driven technologies enable automated interactions across various digital platforms, improving efficiency while maintaining a personalized touch. This chapter explores the role of conversational AI and chatbots in marketing, their applications, implementation best practices, challenges, and future trends.

UNDERSTANDING CONVERSATIONAL AI AND CHATBOTS

Conversational AI encompasses technologies such as chatbots, virtual assistants, and natural language processing (NLP) systems that facilitate human-like interactions. These systems use machine learning, NLP, and data analytics to interpret queries and generate appropriate responses. Key Components of Conversational AI include:

Natural Language Processing (NLP)

Natural Language Processing (NLP) is the foundation of conversational AI. It enables machines to comprehend, analyze, and generate human language in a manner that mimics natural conversation. NLP consists of multiple components, including tokenization, sentiment analysis, part-of-speech tagging, and named entity recognition. These elements help the AI determine intent and provide relevant responses. Businesses benefit from NLP as it allows chatbots to process user queries efficiently, recognize different phrasings, and improve response accuracy over time. By continuously refining NLP models, organizations can create more fluid and intuitive chatbot interactions, improving customer satisfaction and engagement.

Machine Learning (ML)

Machine Learning (ML) plays a critical role in enhancing conversational AI. It allows chatbots to learn from past interactions and adapt their responses based on user behavior and feedback. Unlike rule-based systems, which rely on predefined scripts, ML-powered AI continuously improves by analyzing large datasets. Various ML techniques, such as supervised learning, reinforcement learning, and deep learning, contribute to the development of more intelligent conversational agents. Businesses can train AI chatbots to handle complex queries, predict user needs, and provide more accurate recommendations. ML also enables AI-driven assistants to evolve and enhance their conversational abilities over time, reducing reliance on human intervention.

Context Awareness

Context awareness in conversational AI ensures that interactions remain coherent and meaningful. AI systems achieve this by analyzing previous messages, user behavior, and external data sources to maintain continuity of conversation. Context-aware AI recognizes recurring customers, remembers past interactions, and tailors responses accordingly. This feature is particularly valuable in customer support, where users may seek assistance for ongoing issues. By implementing context awareness, businesses can create more natural and effective chatbot interactions, reducing redundancy and frustration for users. Additionally, contextual AI helps improve personalization by understanding user preferences and adjusting communication style accordingly.

Integration with Business Systems

Conversational AI enhances operational efficiency by integrating with various business systems. These include Customer Relationship Management (CRM) platforms, knowledge bases, e-commerce databases, and ticketing systems. Through seamless integration, chatbots can access relevant information, retrieve order details, assist with transactions, and provide real-time support. Businesses benefit from this connectivity as it enables AI to deliver personalized interactions and expedite problem resolution. For example, an AI-powered assistant integrated with an e-commerce platform can suggest products based on past purchases, answer inventory-related inquiries, and facilitate order tracking. By ensuring robust system integration, companies can optimize customer service while minimizing manual intervention.

KEY APPLICATIONS OF CONVERSATIONAL AI IN CUSTOMER ENGAGEMENT

Customer Support Automation

Customer support automation through conversational AI helps businesses handle customer inquiries effectively. Chatbots serve as the first point of contact for addressing routine questions, troubleshooting issues, and providing relevant information. This automation streamlines support operations, allowing human agents to focus on more complex tasks. Businesses can configure AI chatbots to answer frequently asked questions, guide users through troubleshooting steps, and provide links to resources. Additionally, chatbots can recognize when an issue requires human intervention and escalate the conversation accordingly. Organizations benefit from this technology as it ensures round-the-clock availability and responsiveness, reducing wait times and increasing customer satisfaction. By automating responses to common inquiries, companies can maintain efficiency without compromising service quality. Furthermore, chatbots can be trained to understand various languages, broadening accessibility for global customers. Implementing AI-powered automation reduces the workload on human agents, making customer service operations more manageable and efficient.

Benefits:

- Reducing response times and improving customer satisfaction by offering immediate answers to queries.
- Handling multiple customer interactions simultaneously without affecting performance.
- Offering continuous support, even outside business hours, without incurring additional costs.
- Providing multilingual support to cater to diverse customer bases.
- Streamlining ticketing and case resolution through intelligent routing.

Personalized Customer Interactions

Conversational AI enhances customer interactions by leveraging data to deliver personalized experiences. Chatbots analyze user preferences, purchase history, and prior interactions to provide relevant recommendations and responses. Personalized messaging fosters stronger connections with customers by acknowledging their unique needs. AI chatbots can greet returning customers by name, remember past issues, and offer tailored solutions based on stored information. This customization improves engagement by making interactions feel more natural and user-centric. Businesses can implement AI-driven chatbots that adapt to different user behaviors, ensuring messages resonate with customers. For example, an e-commerce chatbot may suggest products that align with a customer's browsing history, while a banking chatbot may remind users of upcoming bill payments based on their account activity. This level of personalization helps businesses improve customer satisfaction and retention, as individuals appreciate interactions that cater to their preferences. Additionally, sentiment analysis enables chatbots to detect frustration or dissatisfaction, allowing them to adjust responses or escalate interactions when necessary.

Key Features

- Delivering personalized product or service recommendations based on past interactions.
- Customizing greetings and responses to enhance user engagement.
- Remembering previous inquiries to maintain conversation continuity.
- Using sentiment analysis to adjust responses in real time.
- Proactively providing information based on customer needs.

Lead Generation and Qualification

AI-driven chatbots play an essential role in lead generation and qualification by interacting with website visitors, collecting essential details, and assessing potential customers. Chatbots initiate conversations with users, asking relevant questions to understand their needs and interests. By analyzing responses, AI-powered chatbots classify leads based on factors such as intent, budget, and readiness to purchase. This process ensures that sales teams receive high-quality leads, improving conversion rates. Additionally, chatbots provide a seamless way for customers to book appointments, request quotes, or schedule product demos. Businesses can integrate AI-driven lead generation into various digital platforms, ensuring a steady flow of prospective clients. Automated lead qualification reduces the time sales representatives spend on initial inquiries, allowing them to focus on closing deals.

AI chatbots can also nurture leads through follow-up interactions, sending reminders or additional information to guide prospects toward a purchase decision.

Features Include

- Engaging website visitors with interactive conversations that capture attention.
- Asking qualifying questions to assess customer interest and intent.
- Scoring leads based on user responses and likelihood of conversion.
- Automatically scheduling calls or demos with sales representatives.
- Following up with potential leads through email or messaging platforms.

E-Commerce Assistance and Transaction Support

E-commerce businesses utilize conversational AI to enhance the online shopping experience. AI-powered chatbots assist customers throughout their journey by providing product recommendations, answering questions, and facilitating transactions. Chatbots enable users to search for products using natural language, streamlining navigation within e-commerce platforms. Additionally, chatbots assist with checkout processes by guiding users through payment and delivery options. AI-driven chatbots also support cart recovery by sending reminders to users who abandon their shopping carts. This proactive engagement helps businesses recover lost sales and increase conversion rates. Furthermore, chatbots can handle order tracking inquiries, providing real-time updates on shipment statuses. With AI-driven support, e-commerce companies can offer a smoother and more efficient shopping experience, reducing friction and improving customer satisfaction.

Key Benefits

- Offering personalized product recommendations based on browsing behavior.
- Assisting with checkout and payment processes for seamless transactions.
- Sending reminders to recover abandoned carts and improve sales.
- Answering product-related inquiries instantly.
- Providing order tracking and delivery updates in real time.

Multichannel Integration

Conversational AI ensures that customer interactions remain consistent across multiple digital channels. Modern consumers engage with businesses through various touchpoints, including websites, social media, messaging apps, and voice assistants. AI-powered chatbots facilitate seamless communication by integrating with these platforms, allowing users to switch between channels without losing context. For example, a customer might initiate a conversation on a company's website and continue it later via a messaging app. This level of integration improves accessibility and convenience for users. Businesses that implement multichannel AI solutions can engage customers where they are most active, creating a more dynamic and responsive customer experience. Additionally, AI-driven automation in email and SMS enhances communication by delivering timely updates and reminders. By maintaining a consistent presence across digital channels, businesses can provide better support and engagement, fostering stronger customer relationships.

Key Capabilities

- Enabling chatbot interactions on websites, mobile apps, and messaging platforms.

- Integrating with social media channels to provide customer support.
- Offering seamless conversation continuity across different platforms.
- Utilizing voice assistants for hands-free interactions.
- Enhancing email and SMS automation to provide timely updates.

IMPLEMENTING CONVERSATIONAL AI FOR CUSTOMER ENGAGEMENT

Defining Business Objectives

Before deploying conversational AI, businesses should establish clear objectives that align with their strategic goals. These objectives help define the purpose and scope of chatbot deployment while ensuring that AI-driven interactions contribute to overall business success.

Key Objectives:

Improving Customer Support Efficiency | Chatbots can reduce response times by handling routine inquiries, and freeing human agents for more complex cases.

Increasing Lead Conversions | AI chatbots can engage potential customers, answer questions, and guide them through the sales funnel more efficiently.

Enhancing User Engagement | Automated interactions can keep customers engaged through personalized messaging, recommendations, and continuous support.

Clearly defining objectives ensures that businesses choose the right technology, design appropriate chatbot workflows, and set measurable performance indicators. This phase involves analyzing current customer service challenges, identifying opportunities for improvement, and determining how conversational AI can enhance interactions.

Choosing the Right Chatbot Framework

Selecting the right chatbot framework depends on business requirements, target audience, and the complexity of interactions. Different chatbot models cater to various business needs:

Rule-Based Chatbots | These chatbots operate on predefined scripts and decision trees. They work well for structured interactions such as FAQs, appointment scheduling, and order tracking.

AI-Powered Chatbots | Using machine learning and NLP, these chatbots dynamically process queries and generate responses based on user input. They are suited for complex customer interactions, providing more flexible and intuitive conversations.

Hybrid Chatbots | These combine rule-based structures with AI capabilities, ensuring efficiency while allowing AI to handle advanced queries. Hybrid models provide flexibility and adaptability to evolving customer needs.

Businesses should evaluate chatbot frameworks based on their ability to scale, integrate with existing systems, and provide a seamless customer experience. Additionally, considering factors like security, multilingual support, and customization options ensures that the chatbot aligns with organizational needs.

Training Chatbots for Accuracy and Context Awareness

Ensuring that a chatbot delivers accurate and relevant responses requires extensive training. The training process involves feeding chatbots with diverse datasets, refining their understanding of customer queries, and continuously optimizing their learning models.

Essential Training Steps:

Dataset Preparation | Providing the chatbot with structured and unstructured data, including historical customer interactions, product descriptions, and FAQs.

Intent Recognition | Training the chatbot to identify user intents accurately through supervised learning models.

Context Retention | Enabling the chatbot to understand ongoing conversations by maintaining context across multiple interactions.

Testing and Feedback Loop | Conducting rigorous testing to evaluate chatbot responses, gathering user feedback, and refining the AI model accordingly.

Integration with customer databases, CRM systems, and support ticketing platforms enhances chatbot accuracy by allowing it to retrieve relevant information dynamically. Continuous training ensures that the chatbot evolves with changing customer needs and emerging trends in language use.

Seamless Handoff to Human Agents

While AI chatbots improve automation, certain customer interactions require human intervention. Implementing a seamless transition between AI and human agents ensures that customers receive adequate support when needed.

Key Considerations:

Escalation Protocols | Establishing rules that trigger human agent intervention based on the complexity of the inquiry, user sentiment, or escalation requests.

Context Preservation | Ensuring that chatbot interactions are transferred to human agents with full conversation history, preventing users from repeating themselves.

Live Chat Integration | Providing users with options to switch from chatbot to live agent seamlessly, maintaining user experience consistency.

A well-implemented handoff process enhances customer satisfaction by ensuring that AI supports users effectively while allowing human agents to intervene when necessary.

Monitoring and Optimizing Chatbot Performance

Regularly assessing chatbot performance helps businesses optimize interactions, improve customer satisfaction, and refine AI-driven engagement strategies. Monitoring chatbot performance includes tracking key performance indicators (KPIs) and making necessary improvements based on collected data.

Important Metrics to Track:

Response Accuracy | Evaluating how well the chatbot understands and responds to user queries.

User Satisfaction Ratings | Collecting feedback from users to measure chatbot effectiveness and identify areas for improvement.

Chat Abandonment Rates | Analyzing when and why users exit chatbot interactions to enhance engagement strategies.

Resolution Times | Measuring how quickly chatbots resolve user inquiries and escalate unresolved cases to human agents.

Businesses should implement A/B testing to experiment with different chatbot approaches, use analytics tools to gather insights, and regularly update chatbot scripts and training data. Optimizing chatbot performance is an ongoing process that ensures the AI continues to meet customer expectations and business goals.

CHALLENGES IN CONVERSATIONAL AI AND CHATBOT DEPLOYMENT

Understanding Complex Queries

Conversational AI has improved significantly but handling complex and ambiguous queries remains a challenge. Despite advancements in NLP, chatbots sometimes misinterpret user intent, leading to irrelevant or inaccurate responses. Businesses must actively refine chatbot responses to bridge these gaps and improve user interactions.

Key Approaches:

Iterative Learning and Improvement | Businesses should continuously refine chatbot responses based on user interactions, leveraging feedback loops and machine learning models.

Fallback Mechanisms | Implementing fallback options, such as live agent support or alternative response suggestions, ensures that users receive the assistance they need when AI encounters challenges.

Expanding Training Data | Providing diverse and comprehensive datasets during chatbot training can help AI recognize a broader range of customer inquiries and respond more accurately.

Context Retention | AI systems should remember past interactions within a session, allowing for a smoother conversational flow and reducing repetitive queries.

Maintaining a Natural Conversational Flow

A seamless conversational experience is crucial for user engagement. Users expect chatbot interactions to mimic human-like conversations rather than feeling rigid or mechanical. Creating a smooth and intuitive interaction requires thoughtful implementation of language models and sentiment analysis.

Best Practices:

Sentiment Analysis Integration | Implementing sentiment analysis allows chatbots to gauge user tone and adjust responses accordingly. For example, a chatbot recognizing frustration could prioritize empathy in its replies.

Conversational Variability | Avoiding repetitive or overly generic responses by introducing varied phrasings and response structures helps create a more dynamic conversation.

Proactive Engagement | Chatbots can enhance natural conversations by proactively offering relevant information, recommendations, or follow-up questions.

Clarification Prompts | If the chatbot is unsure of user intent, it should ask clarifying questions rather than making assumptions, reducing the likelihood of incorrect responses.

Balancing Automation and Human Touch

Automation enhances efficiency, but a balance between AI-driven interactions and human support ensures a more personalized and effective user experience. Over-reliance on AI can make conversations feel impersonal, while excessive human intervention can slow down responses.

Strategies for Balance:

Human-in-the-Loop Systems | Hybrid approaches allow AI to handle routine queries while seamlessly escalating complex issues to human representatives when needed.

Context-Aware Handoffs | Maintaining the conversation's context when transitioning from AI to human agents prevents users from having to repeat information.

Customizable User Preferences | Offering users the option to interact with a chatbot or request human support upfront can enhance customer satisfaction.

Emotional Intelligence in AI | Programming AI to recognize frustration, confusion, or satisfaction helps determine when to offer human assistance.

Ensuring Data Privacy and Compliance

Conversational AI interacts with sensitive customer data, making data security and regulatory compliance essential. Businesses must implement privacy-focused measures to build customer trust and meet legal requirements.

Key Compliance Measures:

Adhering to Data Protection Laws | Ensuring compliance with regulations like GDPR, CCPA, and other data protection laws applicable to different regions.

Transparent Data Collection Policies | Informing users about how their data is collected, stored, and used fosters transparency and trust.

End-to-End Encryption | Securing data transmission between users and chatbots to protect sensitive customer information.

Data Minimization Strategies | Collect only necessary data and ensure responsible data retention policies.

User Control Over Data | Providing customers with options to delete or modify their data enhances transparency and aligns with privacy regulations.

By addressing these challenges, businesses can deploy more effective conversational AI solutions, improving customer engagement while ensuring compliance and seamless user experience.

FUTURE TRENDS IN CONVERSATIONAL AI AND CHATBOTS

AI-Powered Voice Assistants

Voice-based conversational AI is expected to grow in capability, offering more seamless integration with smart devices. As technology advances, voice assistants will become more context-aware, allowing for more meaningful and dynamic conversations. They will be able to interpret user intent more accurately by analyzing speech patterns, tone, and previous interactions. This will result in more natural interactions that feel less scripted and robotic. Additionally, improvements in multilingual processing will enable voice assistants to cater to a wider audience. Businesses can leverage these advancements to create hands-free customer support options, automate tasks, and provide real-time assistance through voice commands.

Key Developments

- Greater contextual understanding through AI-powered speech analysis.
- Integration with more smart devices for a seamless user experience.
- Improved multilingual processing to serve global audiences.
- Enhanced security measures to prevent unauthorized voice access.
- More dynamic and less rigid response generation.

Advanced Sentiment and Emotion Recognition

Future chatbots will become more effective at recognizing user emotions by analyzing speech tone, word choice, and conversation patterns. By leveraging emotion detection technology, chatbots can adjust their responses in real-time to create more empathetic and effective interactions. For example, a chatbot detecting frustration might switch to a more reassuring tone and escalate the conversation to a human agent when necessary. Businesses can use these capabilities to improve customer experience by ensuring that interactions remain engaging and meaningful. Additionally, AI will be able to measure long-term customer sentiment by tracking interactions over time, allowing businesses to tailor their engagement strategies accordingly.

Expected Enhancements

- More accurate real-time sentiment analysis.
- Context-aware responses that adjust based on emotional cues.
- Integration with customer support systems for intelligent escalation.
- Data-driven insights into customer sentiment over time.
- Improved customer satisfaction through emotionally responsive AI.

Hyper-Personalized AI Chatbots

AI chatbots will continue to evolve by offering highly personalized experiences based on past user interactions and behavioral patterns. Future AI-driven systems will analyze customer data in real-time to deliver tailored responses that match individual preferences. Instead of generic replies, AI chatbots will modify communication styles, tones, and recommendations based on the user's history, making interactions feel more natural and relevant. Businesses will be able to leverage hyper-personalization to provide customized product recommendations, automated reminders, and adaptive conversational flows that align with customer needs.

Key Personalization Improvements

- AI-driven user profiles that adapt over time.
- More precise recommendations based on behavioral data.
- Customized conversation flows that adjust dynamically.
- Increased ability to predict customer needs.

- Integration with loyalty programs to offer personalized incentives.

Integration with Emerging Digital Channels

Conversational AI will expand beyond traditional platforms, integrating with new digital channels such as augmented reality (AR) and virtual reality (VR). Businesses will explore innovative ways to use AI in immersive environments, offering customer service through virtual assistants within AR/VR spaces. In addition, AI-powered chatbots will play a key role in metaverse environments, facilitating transactions, guiding users through virtual spaces, and assisting with interactive experiences. These integrations will redefine customer engagement by creating more interactive and visually engaging interactions.

Key Areas of Expansion

- AI-powered virtual assistants within AR/VR environments.
- AI-driven support for e-commerce transactions in immersive spaces.
- Intelligent chatbot integration with metaverse platforms.
- Enhanced user experiences through interactive AI applications.
- Greater accessibility for users engaging with AI in digital environments.

As conversational AI technology evolves, these advancements will redefine how businesses engage with customers across digital landscapes. Companies that embrace these trends will be well-positioned to create meaningful, dynamic, and efficient customer experiences.

Conversational AI and chatbots have become essential tools for customer engagement, streamlining interactions, automating responses, and improving overall user experience. Businesses leverage these AI-driven solutions to provide instant support, personalize communication, and enhance operational efficiency. By integrating natural language processing, machine learning, and contextual awareness, chatbots can handle a wide range of customer inquiries while maintaining a conversational flow.

Despite the advantages of automation, human oversight remains important for managing complex inquiries, ensuring accuracy, and maintaining a personalized touch. Organizations must balance AI-driven interactions with human support to create a seamless and engaging customer experience. Additionally, businesses must address challenges such as data privacy, sentiment accuracy, and chatbot integration with existing systems to optimize performance.

As technology advances, conversational AI will continue to evolve, incorporating voice assistants, sentiment analysis, hyper-personalization, and integration with emerging digital platforms. These developments will further enhance customer interactions, allowing businesses to engage audiences more effectively across multiple touchpoints. Organizations that embrace and refine AI-driven engagement strategies will be well-positioned to meet changing customer expectations while improving efficiency and scalability in customer support and marketing initiatives.

Key Takeaways

- Core components of conversational AI include Natural Language Processing (NLP), Machine Learning (ML), context awareness, and business system integration.
- Businesses use conversational AI for customer support, personalized interactions, lead generation, e-commerce assistance, and multichannel integration.
- Effective chatbot implementation requires clear business objectives, selecting the right framework, proper training, seamless human handoff, and ongoing performance monitoring.
- Challenges include handling complex queries, maintaining a natural conversational flow, and ensuring data privacy.
- Future trends include AI-powered voice assistants, enhanced sentiment recognition, hyper-personalization, and integration with emerging digital platforms like AR/VR.

Reflection Questions

- How can your business leverage conversational AI to improve customer interactions?
- What challenges do you foresee in implementing AI-driven chatbots, and how can they be addressed?
- How do you see the role of human agents evolving alongside AI in customer support?
- What strategies can ensure a seamless transition between chatbot automation and human intervention?

Action Steps

- Identify three areas in your business where chatbot automation could improve efficiency and customer satisfaction.
- Research different chatbot frameworks (rule-based, AI-powered, hybrid) and determine which aligns best with your business needs.
- Conduct a small-scale chatbot test by integrating a simple AI assistant for FAQs or lead generation.
- Develop a monitoring plan to track chatbot performance using key metrics like response accuracy and user satisfaction.
- Outline a strategy to balance AI automation with human support for complex customer inquiries.

MODULE 11
EMAIL MARKETING AND AI-POWERED AUTOMATION

Email marketing remains a fundamental pillar of digital marketing strategies, offering businesses a direct and effective way to engage with their audience. It helps build relationships, nurture leads, and drive conversions. However, as customer expectations evolve, businesses must adopt more sophisticated strategies to remain competitive.

Artificial Intelligence (AI) has significantly enhanced email marketing by automating processes, optimizing content, improving segmentation, and personalizing communication at scale. AI-powered automation ensures that marketing emails are relevant, timely, and engaging. This chapter explores the role of AI in email marketing, key applications, best practices for implementation, potential challenges, and emerging trends.

THE ROLE OF AI IN EMAIL MARKETING

AI-powered automation has revolutionized email marketing by leveraging machine learning and predictive analytics to analyze customer behavior, anticipate engagement patterns, and optimize message delivery. With AI, businesses can:

Automate email campaigns while maintaining high levels of personalization.

- AI-powered automation enables businesses to send targeted emails at scale without losing the personal touch. By analyzing user behavior, AI ensures that each email sent resonates with the recipient, increasing engagement and interaction.

- AI can craft individualized content by considering factors such as past purchases, browsing history, and demographic details. This level of personalization fosters stronger connections between businesses and customers.
- Additionally, AI-powered automation can segment users dynamically, ensuring that content remains relevant over time. If a user's behavior shifts, AI updates their profile and adjusts the messaging accordingly.

Utilize historical and real-time data to refine segmentation strategies.

- AI enhances traditional email segmentation by examining large datasets and identifying nuanced behavioral trends.
- By continuously analyzing data, AI refines audience segments in real-time, ensuring that subscribers receive content suited to their current interests and needs.
- AI-powered tools leverage predictive analytics to forecast potential customer behaviors, allowing businesses to send preemptive emails that guide users through the sales funnel effectively.

Optimize email timing and frequency to maximize engagement rates.

- Determining the best time to send emails is crucial for engagement. AI analyzes historical open and click-through rates to identify when subscribers are most likely to interact.
- AI dynamically adjusts send times based on each recipient's activity, ensuring that emails arrive at the most opportune moment.

- AI can also prevent over-emailing by determining optimal frequency levels, reducing subscriber fatigue, and minimizing unsubscriptions.

Generate dynamic content that aligns with user preferences and past interactions

- AI-powered email marketing allows businesses to create content that adapts in real-time. Emails can include product recommendations based on past purchases or dynamically update based on user preferences.
- AI analyzes recipient interactions to tailor subject lines, images, and calls-to-action (CTAs) for maximum effectiveness.
- By leveraging AI to craft dynamic content, businesses can create a more engaging and personalized email experience, increasing the likelihood of conversions.

By incorporating AI into email marketing, businesses can significantly enhance efficiency, improve customer experiences, and boost conversion rates.

KEY APPLICATIONS OF AI IN EMAIL MARKETING

AI-Driven Audience Segmentation

Traditional email segmentation methods rely on demographic and behavioral data to categorize audiences. AI takes segmentation a step further by analyzing vast datasets to create highly refined audience groups. This is achieved by utilizing machine learning models that continuously learn from user interactions and behaviors. The segmentation process involves several steps:

Data Collection | AI gathers extensive data points from email interactions, purchase history, website activity, and engagement metrics. This information helps build a comprehensive user profile.

Pattern Recognition | AI identifies user engagement trends and refines segmentation dynamically. It adapts in real-time as customer behavior changes, ensuring the right audience receives the most relevant content.

Predictive Analysis | AI can anticipate future behavior by analyzing historical trends. For instance, if a customer frequently browses a certain category but never makes a purchase, AI can categorize them as a high-intent user and trigger personalized offers or recommendations.

By using AI-driven segmentation, businesses can send highly targeted emails that are more likely to resonate with recipients, leading to higher engagement and conversion rates.

Personalized Email Content

AI-powered personalization goes beyond simply addressing a recipient by name. It enables businesses to create content tailored to individual preferences, improving engagement and fostering stronger customer relationships. Personalization is driven by:

User Behavior Tracking | AI tracks how recipients interact with previous emails, including clicks, opens, and link engagement. Based on this data, AI refines future content to align with the recipient's interests.

Product and Service Recommendations | AI suggests products or services based on past interactions. For example, if a customer previously purchased running shoes, AI may include recommendations for complementary products like athletic socks or fitness trackers.

Lifecycle Marketing | AI ensures that email content aligns with a customer's stage in the sales funnel. A new subscriber might receive educational content, while a long-time customer may get loyalty discounts.

By leveraging AI-driven personalization, businesses can create more relevant and meaningful email experiences for subscribers.

Predictive Send Time Optimization

Sending an email at the right time can significantly impact engagement. AI determines optimal send times by analyzing:

Past Engagement Metrics | AI reviews past open and click-through rates to identify when individual recipients are most likely to engage.

Time Zone Considerations | AI accounts for recipients' geographical locations to optimize send times across different time zones.

User-Specific Behavior | AI can personalize send times for each recipient based on their activity patterns. For example, some subscribers may prefer reading emails in the morning, while others engage more in the evening.

Through predictive analytics, AI ensures that emails reach recipients at the most opportune moment, improving open rates and interactions.

Automated Drip Campaigns

Drip campaigns are pre-designed sequences of emails that are sent based on user actions. AI enhances these campaigns by:

Triggering Based on User Actions | AI monitors user behavior and initiates automated emails based on engagement. For example:

- **Welcome Series** | Sent when a new user subscribes, introducing them to the brand and setting expectations.
- **Abandoned Cart Reminders** | AI detects when a user leaves items in their cart without completing a purchase and sends a reminder email with potential incentives.

- **Re-Engagement Emails** | Sent to inactive subscribers to reignite interest through personalized content or special promotions.
- **Content Customization** | AI adapts email content based on the recipient's engagement with previous emails in the drip sequence.
- **Performance Optimization** | AI continuously evaluates open rates, click rates, and conversions to refine the drip campaign structure.

Automating drip campaigns with AI ensures that recipients receive relevant content at the right stage of their customer journey, improving engagement and conversion rates.

AI-Powered Subject Line and Content Optimization

Email subject lines and content significantly impact open and engagement rates. AI-driven tools enhance these aspects by:

- **A/B Testing at Scale** | AI runs multiple variations of subject lines and content simultaneously to determine the most effective combinations.
- **Sentiment Analysis** | AI evaluates the tone of subject lines and body content to optimize for engagement.
- **Dynamic Content Generation** | AI crafts subject lines and email copy tailored to recipient preferences, increasing relevance and likelihood of interaction.
- **Visual Recommendations** | AI suggests the most effective images, GIFs, or videos to include in emails based on past user engagement data.

By leveraging AI for subject line and content optimization, businesses can create more compelling and impactful email campaigns.

Behavioral Triggers and Email Automation

AI enables real-time email automation based on user actions, ensuring messages are timely and relevant. Common behavioral triggers include:

- **Abandoned Cart Emails** | AI detects when a user adds items to their cart but does not complete the purchase, sending a follow-up email with reminders or incentives.
- **Website Activity Emails** | AI tracks user activity on a business's website and triggers emails based on page visits or searches.
- **Event-Based Emails** | AI sends personalized emails for birthdays, anniversaries, or other milestones, enhancing customer engagement.

Automating these processes with AI ensures that users receive relevant and timely messages, improving their overall experience with the brand.

IMPLEMENTING AI-POWERED EMAIL MARKETING

Selecting AI-Enabled Email Marketing Platforms

To integrate AI into email marketing, businesses must choose platforms that offer AI-driven capabilities such as:

Automated segmentation and audience management | AI-powered segmentation helps businesses create dynamic audience groups based on customer behavior, purchase history, and engagement patterns. Instead of static lists, AI continuously refines segments to ensure the right content reaches the right audience.

Predictive analytics for optimizing send times | AI leverages historical engagement data to determine the best time to send emails, maximizing the chances of recipients opening and engaging with the content.

Personalization engines for tailored content | AI-driven personalization goes beyond addressing recipients by name. It customizes email body content, subject lines, and product recommendations based on each recipient's preferences and past interactions.

Popular AI-powered email marketing platforms include Mailchimp, HubSpot, and Salesforce Marketing Cloud. These platforms integrate AI-driven insights with automation tools, allowing businesses to streamline email marketing efforts while improving effectiveness.

Integrating AI with Existing Marketing Systems

For seamless functionality, businesses should ensure AI-driven email marketing integrates with:

CRM and analytics tools | AI-powered email platforms should sync with customer relationship management (CRM) software to maintain consistent communication and data tracking.

Social media and website activity tracking | AI can analyze user behavior across multiple channels, providing insights that refine email marketing strategies and personalize content based on customer interactions.

Broader marketing strategies | AI-driven email campaigns should align with other marketing efforts, ensuring a cohesive omnichannel experience for customers. Integration with paid ads, content marketing, and social media helps drive consistent messaging across platforms.

By integrating AI into existing systems, businesses can create more targeted, data-driven email campaigns that align with their overall marketing goals.

Ensuring Data Quality and Compliance

AI's effectiveness depends on the quality of data it processes. Businesses must:

Maintain clean and structured email lists | Regularly updating email lists ensures that AI has accurate data to optimize segmentation and personalization. Removing inactive or invalid email addresses helps improve deliverability.

Comply with regulations such as GDPR and CAN-SPAM | Businesses must adhere to email marketing laws, ensuring transparent data collection, providing opt-in options, and including easy opt-out mechanisms.

Provide transparent opt-in and opt-out options | AI-driven personalization relies on customer data, making it essential to offer clear consent options. Ensuring customers understand how their data is used enhances trust and compliance.

Maintaining data integrity and ethical data usage allows businesses to maximize AI-driven marketing benefits while fostering customer trust.

Testing and Refining AI-Generated Email Campaigns

To achieve optimal results, businesses should continuously refine their AI-driven email campaigns by:

Conducting A/B testing on different email elements | AI can test variations of subject lines, email content, and CTAs to determine the most effective combinations for engagement and conversions.

Monitoring key performance metrics | Businesses should track metrics such as open rates, click-through rates, and conversion rates to evaluate AI-driven email effectiveness.

Adjusting AI models based on real-time feedback | AI should be continuously trained using new data. If certain email variations underperform, adjustments should be made based on user behavior and engagement patterns.

By continuously refining AI-powered campaigns, businesses can enhance personalization, engagement, and conversion rates over time.

By expanding AI's role in email marketing, businesses can achieve more precise audience segmentation, improved personalization, and better engagement through optimized send times and automated campaigns. AI-driven innovations continue to evolve, shaping the future of email marketing strategies.

CHALLENGES IN AI-POWERED EMAIL MARKETING

Balancing Automation and Human Touch

Over-reliance on automation can lead to emails that feel detached or overly mechanical, reducing engagement from recipients. To ensure a balance between automation and human touch, businesses should consider the following:

Maintaining a Consistent Brand Voice | Emails should reflect the company's tone and style, ensuring consistency across automated and manually crafted messages. Businesses can achieve this by defining a content style guide that AI-driven tools follow when generating email content.

Personalizing Beyond Names | AI-powered personalization should go beyond inserting the recipient's first name. Emails should reference user preferences, past purchases, or browsing history to create relevant messaging.

Segmenting for Personalization | Rather than using broad automation, segmenting audiences allows businesses to send messages tailored to specific user needs and behaviors. AI can refine these segments over time, making personalization more effective.

Introducing Hybrid Models | A combination of AI-generated content with human oversight ensures that emails retain a natural and engaging tone. Businesses can use AI to draft emails, which are then reviewed and refined by marketing professionals.

Using AI Insights as a Guide | AI can offer recommendations on subject lines, content structure, and engagement timing, but human marketers should assess these insights to ensure they align with brand messaging and customer expectations.

Managing Data Privacy and Security

AI in email marketing requires processing large volumes of user data, making data security and compliance crucial. Businesses should implement the following measures:

Understanding and Adhering to Data Protection Regulations | Compliance with laws such as GDPR, CCPA, and CAN-SPAM is essential. Businesses must ensure that all customer data is collected, stored, and used in accordance with these regulations.

Obtaining Explicit Consent | AI-powered email marketing should be permission-based. Businesses should implement clear opt-in processes where customers knowingly subscribe to email communications.

Ensuring Transparent Data Usage Policies | Businesses must be upfront about how AI-driven email marketing uses customer data. Transparency fosters trust and reassures users that their information is being handled responsibly.

Implementing Strong Data Security Measures | Encrypting customer data, limiting data access to authorized personnel, and regularly auditing security protocols help protect user information from potential breaches.

Providing Easy Opt-Out Options | Customers should have the ability to easily unsubscribe or adjust their email preferences. AI can assist by monitoring opt-out reasons and adjusting email strategies accordingly.

Ensuring AI Accuracy and Relevance

AI models in email marketing require ongoing maintenance to ensure accuracy and effectiveness. Businesses should consider the following approaches:

Training AI with Fresh Data | AI systems must be regularly updated with new customer interactions, purchase behaviors, and engagement trends to refine their predictive capabilities.

Monitoring Performance Metrics | Tracking metrics such as open rates, click-through rates, and conversions helps businesses evaluate AI-generated emails and refine their strategies accordingly.

Avoiding Over-Reliance on AI Predictions | While AI provides valuable insights, human oversight is necessary to ensure content remains relevant. Periodic reviews of AI-generated emails help prevent irrelevant or outdated messaging.

Enabling User Control Over Preferences | Allowing customers to customize their email frequency, content preferences, and topics of interest ensures that AI-generated emails align with user expectations.

Testing AI Models for Continuous Improvement | A/B testing different AI-generated email variations helps refine messaging, optimize engagement, and improve conversion rates over time.

By implementing these practices, businesses can harness AI's potential in email marketing while maintaining relevance, accuracy, and trust with their audience.

FUTURE TRENDS IN AI-DRIVEN EMAIL MARKETING

Hyper-Personalization with AI

Future AI advancements will enable highly refined personalization strategies that focus on individual user behaviors and preferences. AI-driven hyper-personalization involves real-time adaptation of content based on user engagement data, allowing businesses to craft emails that feel highly relevant to each recipient.

Real-time content customization based on engagement data: AI will analyze a user's past interactions with emails, website visits, and previous purchases to deliver content that aligns with their interests. This means two users on the same mailing list may receive entirely different emails, tailored to their unique preferences.

Dynamic email layouts that adjust to individual preferences: Instead of a static email template, AI will dynamically generate layouts that fit an individual's viewing habits. For example, if a user tends to engage more with visually rich content, AI will prioritize images and videos, while another user who prefers reading may receive text-heavy emails.

AI-Powered Interactive Emails

As AI evolves, email marketing will move beyond static content and incorporate interactive elements that enhance engagement. AI will help marketers create emails that encourage real-time user interaction, leading to more meaningful customer experiences.

Embedded surveys and quizzes for real-time feedback: AI will insert tailored surveys, quizzes, or polls within emails, allowing users to engage directly with the content. This provides businesses with valuable customer insights while keeping audiences engaged.

AI-generated videos and animations for enhanced engagement: Rather than using pre-made videos, AI will dynamically generate personalized video content. A recipient might see an animated explainer video tailored to their recent interactions with a brand, making emails more engaging and informative.

Voice-Activated and AI-Powered Email Assistants

With the growing popularity of voice-assisted devices, AI-powered email marketing will expand to accommodate voice-activated interactions. Users will be able to manage their emails, extract key information, and even interact with brands using voice commands.

Email optimization for voice-assisted devices like smart speakers: AI will help structure email content in a way that smart assistants can read them aloud, ensuring accessibility for users who prefer voice-driven interactions.

Smart email sorting and prioritization within inboxes: AI will categorize and prioritize emails based on urgency, content relevance, and user preferences, helping individuals manage their inboxes more effectively.

AI-Driven Conversational Email Marketing

AI chatbots will play an increasingly vital role in email marketing, allowing for real-time interactions and follow-ups based on user engagement. Conversational email marketing will create an ongoing dialogue between brands and customers.

Automated responses based on user interactions: AI-powered chatbots will analyze email responses and provide automated yet contextually appropriate replies. If a user shows interest in a product but has a query, an AI-driven assistant can send a follow-up email addressing their specific concerns.

AI-powered follow-ups and lead nurturing sequences: AI will track how recipients interact with emails and trigger follow-up messages designed to guide them through the sales funnel. These follow-ups will be personalized based on previous engagement, making them more relevant to the recipient.

As AI continues to evolve, these advancements will redefine email marketing, making interactions more dynamic, engaging, and user-focused.

AI-powered automation is transforming email marketing by optimizing segmentation, enhancing personalization, and automating key processes. Businesses that integrate AI-driven strategies can improve customer engagement, refine targeting, and streamline their email marketing efforts based on data-driven insights. By leveraging AI's ability to analyze behavioral patterns, predict engagement, and personalize content, companies can create more relevant and effective email campaigns.

While automation improves efficiency, maintaining a balance between AI-driven interactions and human oversight is essential to ensuring that emails remain engaging and aligned with brand messaging. Businesses must also address challenges such as data privacy, regulatory compliance, and the need for continuous model refinement to maintain accuracy and effectiveness.

Looking ahead, advancements in AI will further shape email marketing, bringing more sophisticated personalization, interactive email experiences, and conversational AI-driven responses. As AI tools continue to evolve, businesses that adopt and refine their AI-powered email marketing strategies will be well-positioned to enhance customer relationships and improve marketing outcomes.

Key Takeaways

- AI-powered automation enhances email marketing by improving personalization, segmentation, and timing.
- AI enables dynamic content generation, allowing emails to adapt based on recipient behavior and preferences.
- Automated drip campaigns and behavioral triggers improve engagement by delivering timely and relevant messages.
- Integrating AI-powered email marketing with existing systems ensures a seamless omnichannel strategy.
- AI will continue evolving, introducing hyper-personalization, interactive emails, and conversational AI-driven responses.

Reflection Questions

- How can AI-powered automation improve your current email marketing strategy?
- In what ways can you personalize email content beyond just using the recipient's name?
- How do you currently determine the best time to send emails, and how might AI improve this process?
- What challenges do you foresee in adopting AI for email marketing, and how can you address them?

Action Steps

- Evaluate your current email marketing strategy to identify areas where AI-powered automation could improve efficiency and engagement.
- Explore AI-enabled email marketing platforms such as Mailchimp, HubSpot, or Salesforce Marketing Cloud to see which fits your needs best.
- Implement AI-driven segmentation by analyzing past email engagement and user behavior data.
- Test AI-driven predictive send time optimization to improve open and click-through rates.
- Set up automated email workflows, such as drip campaigns and behavioral trigger emails, to streamline communication.
- Ensure compliance with data protection regulations by maintaining transparent opt-in and opt-out processes.

MODULE 12
SOCIAL MEDIA MARKETING WITH AI AND AUTOMATION

Social media plays an integral role in modern digital marketing strategies, enabling brands to engage with audiences, distribute content, and drive business growth. With the increasing complexity of managing multiple social media platforms, AI and automation have become essential tools for marketers. These technologies help streamline content creation, optimize ad targeting, analyze engagement metrics, and personalize interactions at scale.

In this chapter, we explore how AI is transforming social media marketing, the key applications of AI-driven strategies, best practices for implementation, common challenges businesses face, and emerging trends that will shape the future of AI-powered social media engagement.

THE ROLE OF AI IN SOCIAL MEDIA MARKETING

AI-driven tools enhance social media marketing by efficiently managing campaigns and providing valuable insights from vast amounts of data. These tools help businesses achieve key objectives such as:

Automating content scheduling and publishing

AI tools streamline the process of scheduling and posting content across multiple platforms. By analyzing engagement patterns, these tools determine the best times to post, ensuring that content reaches the intended audience when they are most active. Additionally, automation reduces the time spent on manual scheduling, freeing up marketers to focus on strategy and creative development.

Identifying trending topics and optimizing content strategies

AI tools monitor social media platforms to detect emerging trends, popular hashtags, and viral content. By leveraging this data, businesses can create timely and relevant content that resonates with their audience. AI can also analyze past engagement data to recommend content formats, themes, and styles that are most effective for specific target audiences.

Enhancing audience engagement with AI-powered chatbots and sentiment analysis

AI-driven chatbots provide real-time responses to user inquiries, improving customer service and engagement. These chatbots are capable of handling common queries, directing users to relevant information, and even assisting with transactions. Sentiment analysis tools assess user emotions and opinions by analyzing comments, reviews, and social media mentions, allowing businesses to tailor their responses accordingly and maintain a positive brand image.

Refining ad targeting and improving bidding strategies for paid campaigns

AI-powered advertising tools enhance ad targeting by analyzing user behavior, interests, and demographics. These tools optimize bidding strategies in real time, ensuring that businesses get the best return on their advertising spend. AI can also test different ad creatives, messaging styles, and placements to determine the most effective combinations for engagement and conversion.

Generating performance insights through social media analytics

AI tools process vast amounts of social media data to provide actionable insights on campaign performance. Marketers can track key performance indicators such as engagement rates, conversion rates, audience demographics, and content reach. These insights enable businesses to refine their social media strategies, improve content effectiveness, and make data-driven decisions that align with business goals.

AI empowers marketers to make data-driven decisions, ensuring that their social media efforts align with audience preferences and behaviors.

KEY APPLICATIONS OF AI IN SOCIAL MEDIA MARKETING

AI-Powered Content Creation and Curation

Creating engaging content consistently is a challenge for marketers. AI simplifies this process by:

Suggesting trending topics based on audience interests. AI tools analyze social media trends, search engine queries, and engagement patterns to recommend relevant topics that resonate with audiences. Businesses can use this data to create content that aligns with current discussions, increasing its reach and engagement.

Generating captions, post copy, and hashtags. AI can analyze language patterns and past engagement metrics to generate effective captions and hashtags. This helps marketers craft compelling messages that align with their brand's voice while optimizing them for better discoverability.

Enhancing visual content with AI-powered image and video tools. AI tools assist in generating and editing visual content by suggesting layouts, adjusting image aesthetics, and even creating graphics. Automated video editing tools can trim, caption, and format content for different platforms, ensuring a polished presentation.

Recommending personalized content for different audience segments. AI enables content customization based on user behavior and preferences. By analyzing past interactions, AI can suggest different content formats, styles, or themes to maximize engagement with various segments.

AI ensures that social media posts remain relevant, engaging, and optimized for performance.

Automated Social Media Scheduling and Management

Managing multiple social media accounts can be overwhelming. AI-driven tools enable marketers to:

Schedule posts at optimal times for maximum engagement. AI analyzes audience activity to determine the best times to publish content, ensuring that posts reach users when they are most likely to interact.

Maintain a consistent posting frequency across platforms. AI tools assist marketers in planning and maintaining a steady stream of content across multiple platforms, reducing gaps in posting and maintaining audience interest.

Automate responses to common queries, improving customer support. AI chatbots and automated response tools handle frequently asked questions, ensuring quick and accurate replies while freeing up human agents for complex inquiries.

Analyze the best performing posts and suggest improvements. AI-powered analytics track post-performance, identifying which content resonates best with audiences. Marketers can use this data to refine their strategies and improve future posts.

These capabilities help brands maintain a strong online presence while reducing manual effort.

AI-Powered Social Listening and Sentiment Analysis

AI enhances social listening by monitoring online conversations about a brand, its competitors, and industry trends. It helps businesses:

Identify positive and negative sentiments in customer feedback. AI processes social media comments, reviews, and mentions to determine overall audience sentiment. This helps brands gauge public perception and respond appropriately.

Detect potential PR crises and address them proactively. By identifying negative trends in conversations, AI tools can alert businesses to potential issues before they escalate. Timely responses can help mitigate damage to a brand's reputation.

Track brand mentions and gauge overall audience perception. AI enables businesses to track direct and indirect mentions of their brand, providing insights into how they are perceived online.

Understand customer pain points and improve marketing strategies. AI analyzes customer feedback to highlight areas for improvement, allowing businesses to adjust their strategies based on audience needs and expectations.

This data-driven approach enables brands to respond to audience needs effectively.

Enhanced Ad Targeting and Optimization

AI-driven advertising allows businesses to maximize their ad budgets by:

Refining audience segmentation based on user behavior. AI analyzes user data, such as browsing habits and past interactions, to segment audiences more accurately and tailor ads accordingly.

Adjusting bids dynamically for better ad performance. AI-powered bidding strategies adjust in real time based on ad performance, ensuring that budgets are allocated efficiently to maximize returns.

Identifying high-performing ad creatives and optimizing campaign elements. AI tools test different ad formats, headlines, images, and call-to-action buttons to determine which elements drive the best results.

Delivering highly personalized ads to target demographics. AI ensures that ads are tailored to specific user interests, increasing engagement and conversion rates.

These AI-powered insights ensure that brands reach the right audience with minimal ad spend wastage.

Chatbots for Social Media Engagement

AI-driven chatbots provide real-time assistance on social media platforms by:

Answering frequently asked questions. AI chatbots can handle a wide range of inquiries, providing users with instant responses and reducing wait times.

Offering personalized recommendations based on user behavior. AI analyzes previous interactions and purchase history to suggest relevant products or content, enhancing the user experience.

Assisting with lead generation and guiding potential customers. Chatbots collect user information and guide prospects through the sales funnel, increasing the chances of conversion.

Enhancing customer support and response time. AI-powered chatbots ensure that users receive prompt assistance, reducing frustration and improving overall customer satisfaction.

Chatbots ensure that brands maintain consistent engagement with their audience while reducing the burden on human support teams.

IMPLEMENTING AI-POWERED SOCIAL MEDIA MARKETING

Selecting the Right AI Tools

Selecting the right AI tools is essential for businesses to streamline their social media marketing efforts effectively. Businesses should evaluate their needs before choosing tools that support:

Content Generation and Scheduling Platforms: AI tools such as automated content creation assistants, post schedulers, and optimization engines help ensure timely and relevant content distribution. These platforms analyze engagement patterns and provide recommendations for optimal posting times.

Social Listening and Sentiment Analysis Tools: AI-powered listening tools track brand mentions, customer sentiment, and trends across social media platforms. They allow businesses to understand public perception and adapt their messaging accordingly.

Ad Optimization and Predictive Analytics Solutions: AI-driven ad platforms analyze performance metrics to optimize budget allocation, refine audience segmentation, and adjust bidding strategies in real-time.

AI-Powered Chatbot Software: Conversational AI tools enhance customer interactions by providing instant responses, guiding users through sales funnels, and assisting with support inquiries.

Choosing the right AI tools enables businesses to enhance efficiency, improve engagement, and drive measurable results in their social media marketing efforts.

Integrating AI with Social Media Strategies

For AI to deliver meaningful results, it must be integrated seamlessly into a brand's social media strategy. Businesses should:

Align AI-Driven Insights with Content Strategies: AI-powered tools provide valuable data on audience preferences, which should be incorporated into content planning to increase engagement and relevance.

Ensure AI Tools Integrate with Existing Marketing Automation Systems: AI should work in conjunction with other marketing technologies, such as CRM software and email automation, to create a cohesive marketing ecosystem.

Leverage AI-Generated Data for Audience Engagement Tactics: AI-powered analytics highlight audience behavior, interests, and sentiment, allowing businesses to personalize interactions and refine engagement strategies.

A well-integrated AI strategy ensures that businesses can maximize the benefits of automation while maintaining a human touch in their social media interactions.

Analyzing AI-Generated Insights for Campaign Optimization

To improve the effectiveness of AI-powered social media marketing, businesses must regularly analyze and refine their strategies. This involves:

Monitoring Key Performance Metrics | AI tools track essential metrics such as engagement rates, reach, impressions, and conversion rates. By evaluating these metrics, businesses can assess the success of their campaigns and make data-driven decisions.

Conducting A/B Testing on AI-Generated Content and Ads | A/B testing helps determine which variations of content and ad creatives perform best. AI can generate multiple versions of content, and businesses can test them to identify the most effective approach.

Adjusting Social Media Strategies Based on AI-Powered Recommendations | AI insights provide suggestions for optimizing content, targeting, and engagement tactics. By acting on these recommendations, businesses can continuously improve their marketing strategies.

Data-driven optimization ensures that businesses stay competitive and adapt their social media marketing approaches based on audience behavior and market trends.

CHALLENGES IN AI-POWERED SOCIAL MEDIA MARKETING

Ensuring Authentic and Human-Like Engagement

While AI enhances automation, it should not replace human interaction. Businesses must:

- Balance AI-driven responses with personalized, human-led interactions by ensuring chatbots and automated responses reflect brand voice and warmth.
- Avoid robotic chatbot interactions that lack emotional intelligence by fine-tuning responses with natural language processing and human oversight.
- Train customer service teams to collaborate with AI tools effectively, ensuring a blend of automation and personal touch in customer interactions.
- Regularly evaluate customer feedback to assess the impact of AI-driven engagements and adjust strategies accordingly.

Managing Data Privacy and Compliance

AI tools rely on user data, making compliance crucial. Businesses must:

- Adhere to regulations such as GDPR and CCPA by ensuring AI-driven data collection and processing align with legal requirements.
- Maintain transparency in AI-driven engagement practices by clearly communicating how user data is collected, stored, and used.
- Implement strong data security measures to prevent breaches and protect user information.
- Regularly review privacy policies to stay up to date with evolving regulations and ensure continued compliance.

Keeping Up with Social Media Algorithm Changes

AI-driven strategies must adapt to platform changes by:

- Staying updated with evolving algorithms that impact content reach through continuous monitoring of platform updates and industry news.
- Adjusting social media approaches based on new trends by testing content variations and analyzing engagement patterns.
- Utilizing AI-powered analytics tools to predict and respond to algorithm shifts effectively.
- Diversifying content strategies to reduce dependence on any single platform's algorithm.

Avoiding Over-Reliance on Automation

AI should support, not replace, human creativity. Brands must ensure that:

- Content remains authentic and aligns with their voice by involving creative teams in the AI content generation process.
- AI-generated insights are reviewed by marketing professionals to maintain quality and relevance.
- Businesses balance automation with manual oversight to ensure content remains engaging and effective.

- AI tools are used as assistants rather than replacements for human creativity in content creation and marketing strategy.

FUTURE TRENDS IN AI-DRIVEN SOCIAL MEDIA MARKETING

AI-Enhanced Visual and Video Content Creation

AI is increasingly transforming the way visual and video content is produced, making it easier for marketers to create engaging, high-quality media without requiring extensive manual effort. This transformation includes:

Automated video editing and captioning tools | AI-powered software can edit videos by identifying key highlights, cutting unnecessary sections, and applying transitions seamlessly. These tools also generate captions, improving accessibility and engagement for a broader audience.

AI-generated visuals tailored for specific audiences | AI can create custom graphics, infographics, and animations based on audience preferences, ensuring that content is both visually appealing and relevant to target demographics. Machine learning algorithms analyze engagement metrics to optimize color schemes, layouts, and visual styles.

Real-time video enhancement and personalization | AI tools can enhance live video streaming by applying real-time filters, background effects, and interactive elements that engage audiences dynamically. Personalization features allow videos to be customized for different viewer segments, maximizing relevance and engagement.

Text-to-video generation | AI systems can convert text-based content into short, visually compelling videos by selecting appropriate visuals, background music, and voiceovers. This innovation reduces the time and resources required for content production, making video marketing more accessible to businesses of all sizes.

Advanced Predictive Analytics for Engagement Optimization

AI-driven predictive analytics is playing a growing role in optimizing social media engagement by forecasting audience behavior and refining content strategies. This application includes:

Predicting audience preferences based on historical data | AI analyzes user interactions, content consumption patterns, and engagement histories to anticipate what type of content will resonate most with specific demographics. By leveraging this information, marketers can tailor their campaigns to meet audience expectations.

Refining posting schedules for maximum reach | AI tools assess when audiences are most active on different platforms and recommend optimal posting times. These recommendations help brands maximize content visibility and audience interaction.

Analyzing sentiment and adjusting messaging | AI evaluates audience sentiment by scanning comments, shares, and reactions to determine how users feel about specific topics. This insight allows brands to refine their messaging, ensuring they align with audience sentiment and preferences.

Identifying potential engagement opportunities | AI detects emerging trends and conversations related to a brand's industry, enabling marketers to participate in relevant discussions and enhance their visibility.

Optimizing content formats and styles | AI-driven analytics help determine whether images, videos, long-form articles, or interactive content perform best with specific audience segments. By adjusting content strategies based on AI insights, brands can improve engagement rates and overall campaign effectiveness.

Integration of AI with Augmented Reality (AR) and Virtual Reality (VR)

AI is advancing the capabilities of AR and VR in social media, providing brands with new opportunities to create immersive experiences for their audiences. Key developments in this area include:

AR filters for interactive brand promotions | AI-powered AR effects allow brands to create unique and engaging experiences on social media. These filters enable users to interact with branded elements, fostering a deeper connection with products and services.

AI-generated virtual influencers engaging with audiences | AI is enabling the creation of digital influencers who engage with audiences in real-time. These virtual influencers can promote brands, share content, and interact with followers, providing a novel approach to influencer marketing.

Personalized virtual shopping experiences | AI-driven AR tools enable consumers to try on products, such as clothing, accessories, and cosmetics, through virtual simulations. These interactive experiences enhance customer decision-making and improve conversion rates.

Enhanced storytelling through immersive content | AI combines with VR to create compelling narratives that allow users to experience brand stories in a highly interactive and engaging manner. This approach enhances brand recall and fosters emotional connections with audiences.

AI-powered gesture recognition for user interactions | AI enhances AR and VR applications by recognizing and responding to user gestures, enabling more natural interactions within immersive environments.

Hyper-Personalized Social Media Ads

AI is making social media advertising more precise and effective by tailoring ads to individual users based on real-time data and behavioral insights. This transformation includes:

Creating micro-segmented campaigns | AI refines audience segmentation by analyzing user behavior, interests, and engagement history. This allows marketers to create highly targeted campaigns that address the specific preferences of different audience groups.

Adjusting ad creatives dynamically for different user groups | AI tools analyze performance metrics in real-time and modify ad elements, such as visuals, copy, and calls-to-action, to improve effectiveness. This ensures that ads remain relevant to different audience segments.

Utilizing AI-driven retargeting strategies | AI enhances retargeting campaigns by identifying users who have interacted with a brand but have not converted. By analyzing browsing patterns and purchase intent, AI delivers personalized ads that encourage users to complete desired actions.

Optimizing budget allocation based on real-time performance | AI-driven algorithms adjust ad spend dynamically to ensure maximum ROI. By shifting budget allocation to high-performing ads and reducing spend on underperforming ones, AI helps marketers optimize their advertising investments.

Incorporating AI-generated ad creatives | AI tools can design ad creatives, generate copy variations, and test different messaging styles to determine the most effective combinations. This streamlines the creative process while enhancing ad engagement rates.

AI and automation are reshaping social media marketing by streamlining content creation, optimizing ad targeting, and enhancing audience engagement. Businesses that integrate AI-driven tools can improve efficiency, personalize interactions, and make data-driven decisions that align with audience preferences. By leveraging AI for social media scheduling, sentiment analysis, and performance tracking, brands can maintain a strong online presence while adapting to evolving user behaviors.

While AI enhances automation, maintaining a balance between data-driven decision-making and human oversight is essential to ensuring that social media interactions remain authentic and engaging. Additionally, businesses must navigate challenges such as data privacy, regulatory compliance, and platform algorithm changes to optimize their AI-driven strategies effectively.

Looking ahead, advancements in AI-powered predictive analytics, AR/VR integrations, and hyper-personalized advertising will further shape social media marketing. Companies that continuously refine their AI strategies while maintaining a human touch will be better positioned to build meaningful connections with their audiences and achieve sustainable growth in the digital landscape.

Key Takeaways

- AI and automation enhance social media marketing by optimizing content creation, ad targeting, and audience engagement.
- AI-driven tools help automate content scheduling, generate insights, and personalize interactions at scale.
- Sentiment analysis and social listening tools allow brands to monitor online conversations and respond effectively.
- AI-powered advertising improves audience segmentation, bidding strategies, and campaign performance.
- While automation increases efficiency, balancing AI-driven interactions with human engagement is crucial.

Reflection Questions

- How can AI tools improve your current social media marketing strategy?
- What aspects of your social media management could benefit most from automation?
- How can you maintain an authentic brand voice while using AI-powered tools?
- What challenges might you face when integrating AI into your social media strategy, and how can you address them?

Action Steps

- Identify and research at least two AI-powered tools that align with your social media marketing goals.
- Conduct a trial run of an AI-driven content scheduler and analyze its impact on engagement metrics.
- Implement a sentiment analysis tool for a week and evaluate audience perception of your brand.
- A/B test AI-generated ad creatives versus manually created ones to determine which performs better.
- Review your current social media analytics and set measurable goals for AI-driven improvements.

MODULE 13
PREDICTIVE ANALYTICS FOR SMARTER MARKETING STRATEGIES

Predictive analytics plays a significant role in modern marketing by leveraging data, statistical algorithms, and AI-driven models to anticipate future customer behaviors, market trends, and business outcomes. Analyzing historical and real-time data allows businesses to make informed marketing decisions, optimize their strategies, and improve customer engagement. This chapter explains the fundamentals of predictive analytics, its applications in marketing, best practices for implementation, challenges businesses may encounter, and future developments in the field.

UNDERSTANDING PREDICTIVE ANALYTICS IN MARKETING

Predictive analytics is a data-driven approach that enables businesses to forecast potential customer actions and market dynamics. The process combines AI, machine learning, and statistical techniques to uncover patterns and generate actionable insights. The key components of predictive analytics include:

Data Collection

Aggregating data from multiple sources such as CRM systems, social media platforms, customer interactions, website visits, and transaction histories. Businesses gather structured and unstructured data from diverse sources, ensuring that relevant customer touchpoints are captured. This data serves as the foundation for predictive models, and companies must consider factors such as data accuracy, completeness, and compliance with privacy regulations when collecting customer information. Modern organizations use automated tools to streamline data aggregation and maintain a centralized database for effective analysis.

Data Processing

Cleaning, structuring, and transforming data to prepare it for analysis. Raw data often contains inconsistencies, duplicates, and missing values, which can affect the accuracy of predictive models. Data processing involves cleaning the dataset by removing errors, standardizing formats, and integrating data from different sources. This stage also includes feature engineering, where relevant variables are created or transformed to improve model performance. Organizations must implement data governance policies to ensure high data quality and consistency before proceeding with analysis.

Statistical Modeling

Using machine learning algorithms and statistical techniques to identify trends and make predictions. Predictive modeling involves selecting appropriate machine learning techniques based on the business objectives and data characteristics. Common approaches include regression analysis, classification models, clustering techniques, and deep learning methods. These models analyze past behaviors, recognize underlying patterns, and generate insights that help marketers understand future customer actions. Companies should conduct rigorous model validation to ensure reliability and accuracy in real-world scenarios.

Actionable Insights

Applying predictive outputs to refine marketing strategies, personalize customer experiences, and optimize advertising efforts. The effectiveness of predictive analytics depends on translating model outputs into actionable business strategies. Marketers leverage insights to develop targeted campaigns, enhance customer segmentation, and improve engagement strategies. Predictive insights also help businesses optimize pricing, determine the best channels for customer communication, and adjust promotional tactics based on anticipated consumer behavior. Organizations should continuously monitor and update predictive models to reflect changing market conditions and maintain relevance in their marketing efforts.

KEY APPLICATIONS OF PREDICTIVE ANALYTICS IN MARKETING

Customer Behavior Prediction

One of the most common applications of predictive analytics is anticipating customer behaviors. By analyzing browsing patterns, transaction histories, and interactions, businesses can:

- Forecast purchase intent and tailor marketing messages accordingly.
- Identify potential high-value customers and design engagement strategies.
- Predict customer churn and develop retention initiatives to minimize attrition.

For example, e-commerce platforms use AI-driven analytics to assess customer browsing habits and suggest relevant products, increasing the likelihood of conversion.

Lead Scoring and Conversion Optimization

Predictive analytics assigns scores to leads based on their likelihood of converting into customers. This enables sales and marketing teams to prioritize efforts more effectively. The process involves:

- Analyzing past interactions, such as website visits, email engagements, and product inquiries.
- Segmenting leads based on demographic and behavioral data.
- Suggesting personalized follow-up actions to nurture high-potential leads.

A data-driven lead scoring approach helps businesses allocate resources more efficiently and improve conversion rates.

Product Recommendations

AI-powered predictive models enhance customer experiences by providing personalized product recommendations. This application benefits businesses by:

- Increasing upselling and cross-selling opportunities.
- Offering tailored recommendations based on real-time browsing behavior.
- Displaying dynamic content on websites, mobile apps, and email campaigns.

Streaming services and online retailers often implement recommendation engines to suggest content and products, keeping users engaged and increasing sales.

Customer Lifetime Value (CLV) Prediction

Predictive analytics helps businesses estimate the long-term value of a customer, allowing them to allocate marketing resources more effectively. CLV prediction involves:

- Analyzing past purchase frequency, order volume, and retention rates.
- Assessing the likelihood of repeat transactions.
- Measuring the impact of loyalty programs on customer engagement and retention.

Understanding CLV enables companies to refine their marketing strategies to focus on high-value customers and foster long-term relationships.

Optimizing Advertising Campaigns

Marketers utilize predictive analytics to improve the effectiveness of paid advertising campaigns. By analyzing audience behavior and ad performance, businesses can:

- Identify high-performing audience segments for precise ad targeting.
- Adjust ad spend dynamically based on real-time engagement data.
- A/B test different ad creatives and optimize messaging for better response rates.

These insights help businesses maximize return on investment (ROI) by delivering the right message to the right audience at the right time.

IMPLEMENTING PREDICTIVE ANALYTICS IN MARKETING

Defining Goals and Objectives

Before adopting predictive analytics, businesses should establish clear objectives. This ensures that predictive analytics aligns with their overall marketing and business strategies. Objectives should be specific, measurable, achievable, relevant, and time-bound (SMART). Common goals include:

Increasing customer retention | Personalized marketing strategies that address individual customer needs and preferences improve engagement and loyalty.

Enhancing lead conversion rates | Businesses can prioritize high-quality leads based on predictive analysis, reducing time spent on low-probability prospects.

Improving ad targeting and campaign performance | Predictive analytics allows for better segmentation, enabling marketers to design campaigns that resonate with specific customer groups.

Defining goals helps businesses focus their predictive analytics efforts effectively. It also provides a basis for measuring success and making necessary adjustments to improve outcomes.

Gathering and Preparing Data

Data quality is a key factor in achieving accurate predictive analytics results. The process of gathering and preparing data involves several essential steps:

Collecting data from diverse sources | Businesses accumulate data from CRM systems, website analytics, customer service interactions, social media platforms, and external third-party sources.

Cleaning and structuring data | Data must be formatted correctly, duplicate entries removed, and inconsistencies addressed to ensure high accuracy.

Ensuring compliance with data privacy regulations | Laws such as GDPR and CCPA regulate how businesses collect, store, and use consumer data. Companies must have clear policies for obtaining customer consent and securing data.

Proper data management ensures that predictive models generate meaningful insights, improving the effectiveness of marketing strategies.

Selecting the Right AI and Machine Learning Models

Different machine learning models support predictive analytics, each catering to specific marketing applications:

Regression Analysis | Useful for forecasting numerical outcomes, such as sales revenue and customer spending trends.

Classification Models | These help segment customers into categories, such as potential buyers, loyal customers, and high-risk churn candidates.

Recommendation Algorithms | Used extensively in e-commerce and content platforms to suggest relevant products or services based on user behavior.

Choosing the right model depends on the business objective and available data. Organizations may also use a combination of models to enhance prediction accuracy and optimize marketing efforts.

Integrating Predictive Analytics into Marketing Platforms

To fully leverage predictive analytics, businesses should integrate it into existing marketing platforms such as CRM, marketing automation tools, and analytics systems. Key benefits include:

Automating decision-making | AI-driven insights help businesses react dynamically to changes in customer behavior.

Personalizing customer interactions | Predictive analytics enables companies to create tailored marketing messages that resonate with individual customers.

Adjusting marketing strategies in real-time | Businesses can optimize their marketing approach by analyzing campaign performance and making necessary changes based on real-time insights.

Proper integration ensures that predictive analytics works seamlessly within marketing operations, improving efficiency and effectiveness.

Testing and Optimizing Predictive Models

Predictive models must be tested and refined to ensure accuracy and relevance. Best practices include:

Conducting A/B testing | Marketers can compare different versions of a campaign to determine which approach yields the best results.

Updating models with new data | As customer behaviors evolve, businesses should update their models with fresh data to maintain prediction accuracy.

Comparing predictions with actual outcomes | Regular performance analysis helps businesses refine their models, ensuring they continue to provide valuable insights.

Continuous monitoring and optimization enable businesses to maintain high levels of predictive accuracy, resulting in better decision-making and improved marketing outcomes.

CHALLENGES IN PREDICTIVE ANALYTICS FOR MARKETING

Data Quality and Availability

Data quality is a crucial factor in predictive analytics, as inaccurate, incomplete, or outdated data can lead to unreliable predictions and flawed marketing strategies. Businesses must establish robust data governance frameworks that include rigorous data validation, cleansing, and enrichment processes. This involves ensuring data consistency across various sources, removing duplicate records, and addressing missing values. Organizations should also prioritize data accuracy by verifying information through automated and manual validation techniques. Furthermore, integrating real-time data streams can enhance predictive models by providing up-to-date insights into customer behavior and market trends. Companies should also implement monitoring mechanisms to regularly assess data quality and address anomalies that may arise over time.

Privacy and Compliance Issues

As data privacy concerns continue to grow, businesses must navigate complex regulatory landscapes. Compliance involves not only adhering to legal requirements but also establishing ethical data collection and usage practices. Companies must ensure transparency in data collection by informing users about how their data will be used and obtaining explicit consent where necessary. Additionally, organizations should implement security measures, such as encryption and anonymization, to protect customer data from unauthorized access. Regular audits and compliance reviews help businesses stay aligned with evolving privacy regulations. Furthermore, companies must balance data privacy with predictive analytics capabilities by leveraging privacy-preserving techniques such as federated learning and differential privacy to enhance security while extracting meaningful insights.

Interpreting and Applying Insights

While predictive analytics generates valuable insights, marketers must be adept at interpreting these findings and translating them into actionable strategies. Effective interpretation requires a thorough understanding of the data sources, the context of the predictions, and the business goals. Marketers should collaborate with data scientists to ensure that model outputs are correctly understood and applied. Additionally, predictive analytics should be used as a guiding tool rather than an absolute decision-maker. Businesses should implement a feedback loop where predictive insights are tested in real-world scenarios, and their outcomes are measured for accuracy. Continuous learning and refinement of predictive models help improve reliability and effectiveness. Moreover, data visualization tools and dashboards can enhance interpretability by presenting complex insights in an intuitive and actionable manner.

Integration with Existing Systems

Seamlessly integrating predictive analytics with existing marketing systems, such as CRM platforms, email marketing tools, and advertising platforms, can be challenging but is essential for maximizing the effectiveness of data-driven strategies. Integration requires technical expertise to ensure smooth data flow across systems while maintaining consistency and accuracy. Businesses should leverage APIs and automation tools to facilitate data synchronization and avoid silos. Additionally, organizations must ensure that employees are trained to use predictive analytics tools effectively within their workflows. Implementing a structured integration approach, including testing and phased deployment, can help mitigate technical challenges. Furthermore, cloud-based analytics platforms offer scalable integration solutions that enable businesses to expand predictive capabilities without significant infrastructure investments. Effective integration ensures that predictive insights are readily accessible and actionable, enabling marketers to optimize campaigns, personalize customer experiences, and improve overall marketing performance.

FUTURE TRENDS IN PREDICTIVE ANALYTICS FOR MARKETING

AI-Driven Predictive Personalization

Advanced AI models will enhance real-time personalization by:

Anticipating customer preferences based on contextual data | AI-driven predictive models analyze past interactions, purchase history, and real-time behavioral data to forecast customer preferences. Businesses can leverage this capability to recommend products, optimize content delivery, and enhance customer engagement. By segmenting audiences based on predictive insights, companies can create more relevant experiences that resonate with specific customer groups.

Delivering tailored experiences at scale | Businesses can implement AI-powered personalization engines that adjust content dynamically based on user preferences. For instance, e-commerce platforms can showcase individualized product recommendations, while media platforms can curate content playlists. This level of personalization enhances customer satisfaction, increases conversion rates, and fosters long-term loyalty.

Automated Decision-Making

Predictive analytics will enable greater automation in marketing decision-making, including:

Adjusting ad budgets dynamically based on performance insights | AI models assess key performance indicators (KPIs) in real-time, reallocating ad spend to high-performing channels. By continuously monitoring engagement metrics, predictive algorithms can optimize budget distribution, ensuring that marketing investments generate maximum return. Businesses can leverage automated bidding strategies to enhance cost efficiency and campaign effectiveness.

Personalizing content across digital channels in real-time | Predictive analytics enables businesses to tailor email marketing, social media posts, and website content dynamically. AI-driven content generation tools analyze customer intent and preferences, adjusting messaging, imagery, and offers based on predictive insights. This approach ensures that customers receive relevant and timely content, improving engagement and conversion rates.

AI-Enhanced Sentiment Analysis

AI tools will improve sentiment analysis, helping businesses understand customer emotions across different channels and refine engagement strategies.

Analyzing social media conversations and customer feedback | Sentiment analysis models evaluate text-based data from social media, online reviews, and customer support interactions. Businesses can track shifts in customer sentiment, identifying potential issues before they escalate and adjusting marketing strategies accordingly.

Refining messaging based on emotional insights | By understanding customer emotions, businesses can craft more empathetic and impactful messaging. AI-powered sentiment analysis helps brands adjust tone, language, and promotional content to align with customer expectations, fostering stronger connections and enhancing brand perception.

Predictive Voice and Visual Search Optimization

As voice and image search trends grow, businesses will optimize content to align with evolving search behaviors using predictive analytics.

Optimizing for conversational search queries | AI-powered analytics can anticipate the intent behind voice searches, enabling businesses to structure content that aligns with natural language queries. Marketers can refine website SEO strategies by incorporating long-tail keywords, question-based content, and structured data that cater to voice-activated searches.

Enhancing visual search capabilities | With the rise of AI-driven image recognition, businesses can optimize product listings and digital assets for visual search. Predictive analytics enables e-commerce platforms to recommend similar products based on image-based searches, improving discoverability and user experience. By leveraging AI-powered tagging and classification, brands can enhance visibility across visual search platforms.

These advancements in predictive analytics will continue to shape marketing strategies, empowering businesses to create more relevant, efficient, and customer-centric experiences.

Predictive analytics provides businesses with valuable insights to improve decision-making, optimize marketing strategies, and enhance customer engagement. By leveraging AI and machine learning, organizations can anticipate customer behaviors, refine targeting efforts, and allocate resources more effectively. These data-driven approaches help businesses personalize customer interactions, improve conversion rates, and maximize return on investment.

Despite its advantages, implementing predictive analytics requires careful consideration of data quality, regulatory compliance, and integration with existing marketing systems. Businesses must establish robust data management practices, ensure transparency in data usage, and continuously refine predictive models to maintain accuracy and relevance.

Looking ahead, advancements in AI-driven personalization, sentiment analysis, and predictive search optimization will further enhance marketing strategies. Businesses that adopt predictive analytics thoughtfully, invest in reliable data sources, and continuously test and optimize their models will be better positioned to create meaningful customer experiences and improve marketing outcomes. As predictive analytics evolves, its role in shaping data-driven marketing strategies will continue to expand, offering new opportunities for businesses to stay competitive in an increasingly digital landscape.

Key Takeaways

- Predictive analytics helps businesses anticipate customer behaviors, optimize marketing strategies, and improve engagement using AI and statistical models.
- Key components include data collection, processing, statistical modeling, and actionable insights.
- Applications include customer behavior prediction, lead scoring, personalized recommendations, customer lifetime value estimation, and ad campaign optimization.
- Successful implementation requires clear objectives, quality data, the right AI models, integration with marketing platforms, and continuous optimization.
- Future trends include AI-driven personalization, automated decision-making, sentiment analysis, and predictive search optimization.

Reflection Questions

- How can predictive analytics help improve your current marketing strategies?
- What challenges might you face in implementing predictive analytics in your organization?
- How can you ensure compliance with data privacy regulations while leveraging customer insights?
- Which predictive analytics application (e.g., customer behavior prediction, lead scoring) would be most beneficial for your business?
- How can you continuously refine and test predictive models to maintain accuracy and relevance?

Action Steps

- Identify specific marketing challenge where predictive analytics could provide value and outline a plan to implement it.
- Assess your current data collection and processing capabilities to determine readiness for predictive analytics.
- Research and evaluate AI and machine learning models that align with your marketing goals.
- Test a small-scale predictive analytics campaign (e.g., lead scoring or personalized recommendations) and measure its impact.
- Create a strategy for ongoing optimization of predictive models, incorporating real-time data and feedback loops.

MODULE 14
AI-DRIVEN PERFORMANCE MEASUREMENT AND MARKETING ANALYTICS

AI-driven performance measurement and marketing analytics are redefining the way businesses evaluate, optimize, and predict the outcomes of their marketing efforts. AI enhances traditional data analysis by automating processes, identifying trends, and providing actionable insights. With AI-powered tools, marketers can monitor campaigns in real time, improve customer segmentation, and allocate budgets more efficiently. This chapter explores how AI improves marketing analytics, the key applications of AI-driven performance measurement, best practices for implementation, challenges, and future trends in AI-driven marketing analytics.

THE ROLE OF AI IN MARKETING ANALYTICS

The use of AI in marketing analytics is transforming the industry by offering businesses a more efficient and intelligent way to manage data and make informed decisions. AI enables companies to analyze large datasets, detect patterns, and provide real-time insights. Here are some of the key functions of AI in marketing analytics:

Automating Data Collection and Processing

- AI tools can aggregate data from multiple sources, such as social media, CRM systems, website analytics, and sales data, enabling businesses to have a holistic view of marketing performance.

- Machine learning algorithms can process structured and unstructured data, extracting valuable insights from textual data, images, and videos.
- AI-driven automation reduces manual effort in data collection, ensuring accuracy and consistency in reporting.
- Data cleaning and normalization techniques powered by AI help eliminate errors, standardize formats, and enhance the reliability of analytics.
- AI facilitates faster data integration, making real-time updates accessible for more informed marketing decisions.
- AI-based data visualization tools create interactive dashboards that present data intuitively, making insights more actionable.
- Advanced AI models can link disparate data points to generate comprehensive performance overviews, helping businesses identify gaps and opportunities.

Enhancing Customer Insights

- AI identifies behavioral trends and customer preferences by analyzing historical and real-time data.
- Advanced analytics help businesses tailor marketing strategies to align with audience expectations and improve engagement rates.
- AI-driven sentiment analysis enables businesses to understand customer emotions, providing a deeper layer of insight into engagement patterns.
- AI-powered chatbots and virtual assistants collect customer interaction data, helping marketers personalize future communications.

- Predictive analytics models assess customer lifetime value, guiding businesses in nurturing and retaining high-value customers.
- AI-based recommendation engines enhance personalization by suggesting products or content tailored to individual user preferences.
- Social listening tools leverage AI to analyze brand mentions and consumer conversations, allowing businesses to adjust marketing messaging in response to emerging trends.

Predicting Marketing Performance

- AI models use historical data to forecast the success of marketing campaigns, allowing marketers to adjust their strategies proactively.
- Predictive analytics help businesses anticipate customer responses, making it easier to allocate resources efficiently.
- AI can analyze past purchasing behavior and browsing patterns to predict future buying trends, helping companies create demand-driven marketing strategies.
- Machine learning algorithms assess seasonal patterns and external factors, enabling businesses to prepare for fluctuations in customer demand.
- AI-driven forecasting models can simulate different marketing scenarios, helping companies evaluate potential risks and opportunities before execution.
- AI refines marketing mix modeling, identifying the most effective combination of channels, messages, and timing for campaign success.

- Businesses can use AI-powered churn prediction models to identify at-risk customers and implement retention strategies before losing them.

Optimizing Marketing ROI

- AI-powered analytics provide insights into which channels, messages, and timing yield the highest return on investment (ROI).
- AI continuously refines marketing strategies based on new data, ensuring long-term campaign success.
- AI-driven budget allocation tools analyze past performance and current trends to recommend optimal spending strategies.
- AI enhances customer journey mapping by identifying key touchpoints and interactions that contribute to conversions.
- Dynamic pricing strategies powered by AI help businesses optimize pricing structures based on real-time demand and competitor behavior.
- AI assists in real-time ad bidding optimization, ensuring businesses allocate advertising spend efficiently for maximum ROI.
- AI-driven marketing attribution models provide a clear picture of which channels contribute most to sales, allowing businesses to refine investment strategies effectively.

KEY APPLICATIONS OF AI IN PERFORMANCE MEASUREMENT

AI enhances performance measurement by providing marketers with real-time insights, predictive analytics, and automation capabilities. The following applications highlight the role of AI in marketing performance evaluation:

Real-Time Marketing Analytics

AI enables businesses to monitor marketing performance in real time, allowing for immediate adjustments to improve outcomes.

- Tracks website traffic, user interactions, and social media engagement, ensuring businesses can analyze audience behavior as it unfolds.
- Analyzes conversion rates by monitoring various digital touchpoints, helping businesses understand which aspects of their campaigns drive customer actions.
- Provides instant feedback on campaign effectiveness, allowing for timely modifications, whether in ad placement, content strategy, or promotional offers.
- AI-powered sentiment analysis can evaluate customer feedback in real-time, allowing companies to pivot marketing strategies based on public perception.
- Dynamic pricing models can adjust prices in real-time based on customer demand, competitor pricing, and purchasing trends.
- AI-driven chatbots and virtual assistants can analyze customer inquiries and responses, providing insights into common concerns or interests.
- Real-time heatmaps and engagement tracking help businesses optimize web design and content layout based on user behavior.

AI-Driven Customer Segmentation Analytics

AI helps marketers refine audience segmentation by analyzing customer behavior and engagement patterns.

- Identifies high-value customer segments by analyzing purchasing behavior, website activity, and demographic data.
- Uses predictive modeling to anticipate customer actions, helping businesses craft personalized offers and recommendations.
- Adjusts marketing efforts dynamically, ensuring that advertisements, email campaigns, and promotions are aligned with changing customer preferences.

- AI-powered segmentation enables hyper-targeted marketing by analyzing behavioral cues such as browsing history, previous purchases, and social media interactions.
- Sentiment analysis enhances segmentation by grouping customers based on emotional engagement with products and services.
- AI helps in identifying emerging customer segments by detecting trends in purchasing habits and new customer acquisition patterns.
- Marketers can leverage AI-driven insights to create adaptive customer journeys, ensuring a more personalized experience at each stage of interaction.

Predictive Analytics for Marketing Performance

AI-powered predictive analytics allow businesses to anticipate future marketing trends and optimize their campaigns accordingly.

- Analyzes past marketing campaign data to forecast future engagement trends, helping marketers make informed decisions about upcoming initiatives.
- Helps businesses understand how customers may respond to different advertising strategies by simulating potential outcomes based on historical data.
- Supports data-driven decision-making, reducing reliance on intuition and guesswork in crafting marketing strategies.
- AI-driven predictive models can optimize content marketing by forecasting the types of content that will generate the most engagement.
- AI can predict shifts in consumer demand based on macroeconomic factors, enabling businesses to prepare marketing strategies accordingly.
- AI-driven competitor analysis helps businesses predict market movements and adjust marketing campaigns to remain competitive.

- AI models can refine email marketing campaigns by predicting the best times to send emails, the most engaging subject lines, and the likelihood of conversions.

AI-Powered Attribution Modeling

Understanding which marketing channels contribute most to conversions is essential for effective budget allocation.

- AI-driven attribution models assess the impact of different touchpoints in the customer journey, helping businesses determine the effectiveness of their marketing strategies.
- Provides detailed insights into channel performance, allowing businesses to allocate marketing budgets more efficiently based on conversion data.
- Enhances understanding of customer pathways, improving multi-channel marketing strategies and optimizing the customer experience.
- AI-driven multi-touch attribution models evaluate how various channels (social media, email, organic search, paid ads) work together in generating conversions.
- AI-powered customer journey mapping helps businesses visualize how consumers interact with different marketing assets before making a purchase.
- AI assists in reducing attribution bias by considering non-traditional factors such as offline interactions, word-of-mouth influence, and indirect touchpoints.
- Advanced attribution models incorporate sentiment analysis, helping businesses assess not only conversion rates but also the emotional impact of different touchpoints.

Automated A/B Testing and Campaign Optimization

AI enhances A/B testing by enabling marketers to test multiple variations of campaigns simultaneously.

- AI-driven testing tools analyze results in real-time, accelerating the decision-making process and optimizing marketing efforts more efficiently.
- Optimizes elements such as messaging, visuals, and targeting criteria by analyzing real-time user responses and continuously improving the campaign's effectiveness.
- Eliminates the need for manual analysis by automating testing, reducing the time and resource investment required for experimentation.
- AI-powered A/B testing can simultaneously test multiple factors such as color schemes, ad placements, call-to-action buttons, and audience segments.
- AI models automatically adjust underperforming elements and allocate more resources to the highest-performing variations.
- Predictive AI-driven testing forecasts the impact of changes before full deployment, reducing the risk of ineffective campaign rollouts.
- AI helps analyze A/B test data at a granular level, identifying patterns in user interactions that may not be immediately visible through traditional analysis.

IMPLEMENTING AI IN MARKETING PERFORMANCE MEASUREMENT

To effectively integrate AI into marketing analytics, businesses should consider the following steps:

Choosing AI-Powered Analytics Tools

Selecting the right AI-driven analytics platform is crucial for seamless integration and actionable insights. Businesses must evaluate AI solutions based on their specific needs and operational goals.

Opt for platforms that offer data integration from various marketing channels. AI tools should be capable of aggregating and analyzing data from multiple sources such as social media, website interactions, and customer relationship management (CRM) systems. The ability to unify data sources ensures a comprehensive view of marketing performance.

Look for tools that provide predictive analytics and real-time reporting capabilities. AI-driven predictive analytics can anticipate market trends and customer behaviors, helping businesses make informed decisions. Real-time reporting capabilities allow for immediate course corrections, ensuring marketing strategies remain effective.

Ensure customizable dashboards to track performance based on specific business goals. Businesses should prioritize platforms that offer user-friendly interfaces and adaptable dashboards, allowing teams to visualize data in ways that align with key performance indicators (KPIs).

Evaluate scalability and adaptability. As businesses grow, their marketing needs will evolve. AI tools should be flexible enough to scale with expanding data requirements and adapt to new trends in the industry.

Assess automation and workflow capabilities. AI-driven automation should streamline routine processes, such as campaign performance analysis and reporting, to enhance efficiency and reduce manual workloads.

Consider security and compliance features. Marketing analytics tools should comply with data protection regulations such as GDPR and CCPA, ensuring that customer data is handled responsibly and securely.

Integrating AI Analytics with Marketing Platforms

A successful AI-driven marketing strategy requires the seamless integration of AI analytics tools with existing marketing platforms. Businesses must ensure compatibility and synchronization for optimal performance.

AI should integrate with CRM, email marketing, and social media management platforms. This integration ensures that businesses can track customer journeys across multiple touchpoints, improving engagement strategies and personalization efforts.

Data synchronization ensures a unified view of marketing performance, reducing data silos. Many organizations struggle with fragmented data across different systems. AI tools should enable data harmonization, ensuring marketers have a complete and coherent dataset for analysis.

AI insights should be leveraged to enhance marketing automation efforts. AI can identify trends and trigger automated responses, such as sending personalized email campaigns based on customer behavior. AI-driven automation improves efficiency and reduces human intervention in repetitive tasks.

Adopt API-driven solutions for easier integration. AI tools with robust APIs allow seamless data exchange between marketing platforms, improving workflow automation and reducing reliance on manual data entry.

Enable cross-functional collaboration. AI-driven analytics should be accessible to multiple departments, including marketing, sales, and customer service, ensuring that insights are utilized across the organization.

Regularly assess integration effectiveness. Businesses should periodically evaluate the performance of AI-integrated tools, ensuring that they continue to provide accurate and valuable insights.

Leveraging AI for Data-Driven Decision-Making

Businesses should utilize AI-powered insights to make informed marketing decisions. AI's ability to process large datasets and identify patterns enables organizations to optimize their strategies based on data rather than assumptions.

AI can identify high-performing content and suggest optimal ad placements. By analyzing engagement metrics and conversion rates, AI tools can determine which types of content and ad placements resonate most with target audiences.

Helps allocate budgets effectively based on historical and real-time data. AI-driven budget allocation models assess past performance and real-time trends to optimize spending across various marketing channels.

Provides continuous performance monitoring for ongoing campaign improvements. AI enables real-time tracking of marketing campaigns, allowing businesses to refine their strategies dynamically. For instance, if an ad campaign underperforms, AI can recommend adjustments to improve engagement.

Facilitates customer sentiment analysis. AI can assess social media conversations, customer reviews, and survey responses to gauge public perception of a brand or campaign, helping businesses make data-driven adjustments.

Enhance segmentation and targeting efforts. AI can analyze consumer behavior patterns, segment audiences more precisely, and tailor marketing efforts to specific demographics and preferences.

Supports long-term strategy development. AI-driven analytics provide insights into macro trends, allowing businesses to make informed long-term strategic decisions rather than focusing solely on short-term campaign performance.

Encourages agility in marketing operations. AI's ability to detect changes in consumer behavior and market trends enables businesses to pivot quickly and adapt their marketing efforts as needed.

By following these steps, businesses can ensure that AI is effectively integrated into their marketing analytics strategies, leading to more precise decision-making, improved performance tracking, and better overall marketing outcomes.

CHALLENGES IN AI-DRIVEN MARKETING ANALYTICS

While AI provides significant advantages, businesses must navigate certain challenges to maximize its benefits.

Ensuring Data Accuracy and Reliability

AI-driven insights depend on high-quality data. The effectiveness of AI-powered analytics is largely determined by the quality and reliability of the data it processes.

Data Validation and Cleaning | Businesses should implement data validation and cleaning processes to maintain accuracy. This includes removing duplicates, correcting inconsistencies, and standardizing data formats.

Regular Data Updates | Keeping datasets updated ensures relevance and improves AI-driven predictions. Outdated or incomplete data can lead to misleading insights, affecting marketing decisions.

Handling Data Gaps | Missing or incomplete data can impact AI models. Businesses should use imputation techniques to fill gaps and enhance predictive accuracy.

Avoiding Data Bias | AI models can inherit biases present in historical data. Businesses must ensure that training datasets are diverse and representative of all customer segments.

Human Oversight in AI Decision-Making | Regular human intervention is necessary to cross-check AI-generated insights and verify their accuracy.

Quality Data Sourcing | Businesses should use reliable data sources, ensuring that data collection processes align with industry standards.

Balancing AI Insights with Human Expertise

AI can offer recommendations, but human judgment is still essential for strategic decisions. Relying solely on AI-generated insights without human interpretation can lead to incomplete or misaligned marketing strategies.

Complementing AI with Human Expertise | AI-driven analytics should assist rather than replace human decision-making. Marketers should critically assess AI insights before acting upon them.

Understanding AI Recommendations | AI provides statistical probabilities and correlations, but human expertise is needed to interpret these in the context of business goals and market dynamics.

Avoiding Over-Reliance on AI | While AI can automate tasks, certain creative and strategic decisions require human intuition and industry experience.

Ethical Considerations in AI Decision-Making | AI models do not possess ethical reasoning. Businesses should ensure that AI-driven marketing decisions align with ethical standards and brand values.

Training Teams on AI Utilization | Businesses should invest in training programs to educate marketing teams on how to integrate AI insights effectively into decision-making.

Managing Data Privacy and Compliance

AI analytics require handling sensitive customer data, making compliance with regulations critical. The increasing use of AI in marketing raises concerns about data privacy and security.

Adhering to Data Protection Laws | Businesses must ensure compliance with data regulations such as GDPR, CCPA, and other local privacy laws.

Implementing Transparent Data Collection Practices | Customers should be informed about how their data is being collected and used.

Securing Customer Information | AI tools should have robust encryption and security measures in place to protect sensitive customer data from breaches and unauthorized access.

Data Anonymization and Minimization | Businesses should adopt practices such as anonymizing data to reduce privacy risks while still leveraging AI for analytics.

Building Customer Trust | Transparency in data usage fosters customer trust and strengthens brand credibility.

Regular Compliance Audits | Businesses should conduct routine audits to ensure AI tools and data handling practices adhere to evolving regulatory standards.

Adapting to Changing AI Models and Algorithms

AI models continue to evolve, requiring businesses to stay informed about updates and improvements. The dynamic nature of AI-driven tools necessitates ongoing adaptation.

Continuous Monitoring and Optimization | Regular evaluation of AI-powered analytics tools is essential to ensure they provide accurate and relevant insights.

Understanding AI Model Changes | As AI models update, their outputs may shift. Marketers should track these changes and adjust strategies accordingly.

Investing in AI Training and Skill Development | Businesses should provide ongoing training to marketing teams, equipping them with the knowledge to adapt to evolving AI trends.

Ensuring AI Model Transparency | Marketers should have visibility into how AI models generate insights to avoid blindly following opaque algorithms.

Testing and Validating AI Outputs | Businesses should validate AI-generated recommendations against real-world results to assess accuracy and effectiveness.

Balancing Innovation with Stability | While adopting new AI tools can provide competitive advantages, businesses should ensure a stable transition to avoid disrupting existing marketing operations.

By addressing these challenges, businesses can maximize the potential of AI in marketing analytics while mitigating risks and ensuring responsible AI implementation.

FUTURE TRENDS IN AI-DRIVEN MARKETING ANALYTICS

AI will continue to shape the future of marketing analytics with emerging technologies and innovations. As AI advances, businesses will be able to leverage increasingly sophisticated tools to enhance predictive capabilities, sentiment analysis, real-time dashboards, and IoT integration. The following sections explore these key future trends in depth.

AI-Enhanced Predictive Analytics

AI-driven predictive analytics will play a crucial role in shaping future marketing strategies. Businesses will rely more heavily on AI models to anticipate customer behavior, optimize advertising efforts, and allocate resources efficiently.

Refining Customer Behavior Predictions | AI models will continuously improve in understanding individual consumer preferences and predicting purchasing behaviors based on past interactions, social signals, and contextual factors.

Improving Personalization in Marketing | AI-powered systems will enable businesses to create highly customized marketing messages by predicting what content or offers resonate best with specific customer segments.

Enhancing Forecasting Accuracy | Future predictive analytics will integrate more diverse data sources, such as economic indicators, social sentiment, and weather patterns, to provide more comprehensive insights into market trends.

Dynamic Campaign Adjustments | AI models will enable businesses to automatically adjust campaigns based on predicted engagement levels, maximizing conversion rates while minimizing wasted marketing spend.

Adapting to Emerging Market Trends | AI-driven forecasting will help companies identify shifts in consumer interests and proactively refine marketing strategies to align with changing preferences.

AI-Driven Sentiment Analysis for Brand Monitoring

Sentiment analysis powered by AI will become an essential tool for understanding consumer perceptions and managing brand reputation in real-time.

Monitoring Social Media and Online Reviews | AI-driven sentiment analysis tools will enable businesses to track customer sentiment across multiple channels, including social media, forums, and product reviews.

Detecting Brand Reputation Risks | Advanced AI models will identify potential reputation risks before they escalate by analyzing trends in customer feedback, flagging negative sentiments, and predicting the potential impact on brand perception.

Enhancing Customer Engagement Strategies | AI-powered sentiment analysis will provide businesses with real-time feedback on how their campaigns and customer interactions are perceived, allowing them to make immediate adjustments.

Automating Crisis Management Responses | AI will help businesses respond to emerging PR crises by generating data-driven insights and recommendations on the most effective course of action.

Understanding Emotional Triggers in Marketing | AI-driven analysis of customer language and tone will help businesses create more emotionally resonant marketing messages, improving engagement and brand loyalty.

AI-Powered Marketing Dashboards

The next generation of AI-powered marketing dashboards will provide more interactive and intelligent data visualization, enabling marketers to make data-driven decisions more effectively.

Real-Time Performance Tracking | AI-driven dashboards will offer continuously updated insights into key marketing metrics, allowing businesses to make informed decisions instantly.

Automating Data Interpretation | Instead of requiring manual analysis, AI-powered dashboards will automatically highlight important trends, anomalies, and areas that require attention.

Customizable Reports Based on Business Goals | AI will tailor reports to align with specific marketing objectives, helping different teams access the most relevant insights for their roles.

AI-Assisted Decision Making | AI-powered dashboards will not only present data but also offer actionable recommendations on campaign adjustments, budget allocation, and customer engagement strategies.

Seamless Integration with Other Business Systems | AI dashboards will integrate with sales, CRM, and customer support platforms to provide a holistic view of customer interactions and marketing performance.

Integration of AI with IoT for Marketing Insights

As IoT devices become more widespread, AI will increasingly integrate with these technologies to gather real-time consumer insights and enhance marketing efforts.

Tracking Real-Time Customer Interactions | AI-powered IoT devices, such as smart displays and connected retail solutions, will collect and analyze data on in-store customer behaviors and preferences.

Enhancing Personalization in Physical Retail Spaces | IoT-connected AI systems will allow businesses to deliver personalized promotions and product recommendations to customers in real-time based on their browsing and purchasing history.

Gathering Behavioral Data from Wearable Technology | AI will analyze data from wearable devices to understand consumer habits and tailor marketing strategies accordingly.

Optimizing Supply Chain and Inventory Management | AI-driven IoT analytics will provide businesses with insights into product demand, enabling more efficient supply chain management and reducing instances of stock shortages or overstocking.

Leveraging Smart Assistants for Marketing Engagement | AI-powered virtual assistants and smart home devices will become an essential part of marketing strategies, helping businesses interact with consumers in new and innovative ways.

AI-driven performance measurement and marketing analytics provide businesses with a data-driven approach to evaluating and optimizing their marketing strategies. By leveraging AI-powered tools, companies can streamline data collection, enhance customer segmentation, predict campaign performance, and improve budget allocation. These insights help marketers make informed decisions, refine messaging, and adapt strategies in real time.

While AI enhances efficiency, businesses must ensure data accuracy, maintain compliance with privacy regulations, and balance automation with human expertise. Addressing these challenges allows companies to maximize the benefits of AI while maintaining responsible and ethical marketing practices.

Looking ahead, advancements in predictive analytics, sentiment analysis, AI-powered dashboards, and IoT integration will further refine marketing analytics. Companies that continuously adapt to these developments and integrate AI strategically will gain deeper insights, improve engagement, and optimize their marketing efforts in an increasingly data-driven landscape.

Key Takeaways

- AI-driven customer insights help businesses tailor strategies based on behavioral patterns, sentiment analysis, and predictive modeling.
- Predictive analytics enables businesses to anticipate marketing performance, optimize resource allocation, and refine targeting.
- AI improves return on investment (ROI) by continuously analyzing campaign performance and adjusting strategies in real-time.
- AI-driven attribution models provide a clearer picture of which marketing channels contribute most to conversions. Future trends include AI-powered predictive analytics, sentiment analysis for brand monitoring, intelligent marketing dashboards, and IoT integration.

Reflection Questions

- What marketing decisions could benefit from predictive analytics, and how might AI improve forecasting accuracy?
- In what ways could AI-driven customer segmentation refine your target audience?
- How does your company ensure data accuracy and compliance with privacy regulations in marketing analytics?
- What challenges do you foresee in adopting AI-powered marketing tools, and how could you address them?

Action Steps

- Review existing marketing analytics platforms to determine if AI-powered solutions could improve efficiency and insights.
- Explore AI-driven tools that refine audience targeting through behavioral analysis and sentiment tracking.
- Identify key areas where AI could enhance forecasting and optimize marketing spend.
- Establish processes for data cleaning, validation, and normalization to ensure reliable AI-driven insights.
- Regularly evaluate AI-driven analytics to adjust strategies and align with evolving market conditions.

PART V
THE ROAD AHEAD

MODULE 15
THE FUTURE OF AI, MARTECH, AND AUTOMATION IN DIGITAL MARKETING

Preparing for the Future of Marketing is essential, as digital marketing is transforming through AI, MarTech, and automation, reshaping strategies for the future. These innovations are reshaping how businesses connect with customers, refine marketing strategies, and leverage data to improve decision-making. As AI and automation become increasingly integrated into marketing workflows, they offer businesses greater efficiency, deeper personalization, and enhanced adaptability. This chapter delves into the evolving role of AI in digital marketing, emerging trends, challenges, and future opportunities.

THE EVOLVING ROLE OF AI IN DIGITAL MARKETING

AI has already demonstrated its potential to revolutionize digital marketing by enabling personalized customer interactions, automating repetitive processes, and supporting data-driven decision-making. As AI technology advances, it will play a growing role in the following areas:

Customer Interaction

AI-driven chatbots and conversational interfaces have transformed customer engagement, allowing businesses to provide real-time, 24/7 support. These AI-powered solutions can handle frequently asked questions, troubleshoot issues, and guide customers through purchase decisions. AI-driven sentiment analysis helps brands gauge customer emotions and tailor responses accordingly. Additionally, the integration of AI with voice assistants is making interactions more intuitive, enabling hands-free, voice-based customer service.

Content Generation

AI-powered tools are increasingly used to create diverse forms of content, from blog articles to product descriptions and social media posts. Natural language processing (NLP) models can generate coherent, contextually relevant text, reducing the workload for content creators. AI can also aid in video and image generation, automating the creation of marketing visuals. By analyzing audience engagement, AI can suggest content modifications, ensuring that brands produce material that resonates with their target demographics.

Predictive Analytics

Predictive analytics, powered by AI, is enhancing marketing decision-making by analyzing historical data to forecast trends and consumer behavior. AI-driven insights help businesses identify high-value customers, anticipate purchasing patterns, and personalize marketing campaigns. By leveraging machine learning algorithms, companies can refine targeting strategies, optimize advertising spend, and adjust pricing dynamically based on market trends and competitor activity.

Marketing Automation

AI-driven automation is streamlining marketing operations, improving efficiency and consistency. Businesses use AI-powered email marketing platforms to segment audiences, personalize content, and determine optimal send times. AI enhances social media management by automating post scheduling, content curation, and audience interaction. In digital advertising, AI optimizes ad placements, bidding strategies, and audience targeting, ensuring maximum return on investment (ROI). Marketing automation enables brands to focus on strategy and creativity while reducing the burden of repetitive tasks.

KEY TRENDS IN AI, MARTECH, AND AUTOMATION

Hyper-Personalization in Marketing

AI-driven personalization is transforming how businesses engage with customers by offering tailored experiences based on individual preferences, behaviors, and interactions. This method allows companies to create a more relevant and engaging experience for their audience.

Real-time Customization of Website Content | AI tools analyze user behavior, such as browsing habits, previous purchases, and time spent on certain pages, to dynamically adjust website content. This includes displaying personalized product recommendations, targeted banners, and customized messaging that aligns with user interests.

AI Analysis of Browsing History, Past Purchases, and Interactions | AI-driven analytics tools assess historical customer data to refine marketing messages and predict future behaviors. This helps businesses craft more compelling offers, ensuring that users receive the most relevant promotions and content.

AI-Powered Product Recommendations Based on Behavioral Predictions | By utilizing machine learning models, businesses can offer predictive recommendations tailored to customer preferences. AI systems analyze shopping habits, search queries, and engagement with similar products to present items most likely to interest the consumer.

With AI's growing capabilities, brands can continuously refine their personalization strategies, enhancing engagement and fostering long-term customer loyalty.

AI-Powered Conversational Marketing

Conversational AI is increasingly integral to modern marketing strategies, offering businesses new ways to interact with customers through natural and meaningful exchanges.

AI Chatbots with Contextual Awareness | AI-driven chatbots are now capable of handling more sophisticated customer queries by understanding context and sentiment. This enables brands to provide accurate, timely responses that improve customer satisfaction and streamline support services.

Voice Assistants for Voice-Based Interactions | The rise of voice assistants such as Alexa, Google Assistant, and Siri has encouraged businesses to optimize their content and customer interactions for voice search. AI-powered voice interfaces allow consumers to place orders, receive recommendations, and get real-time assistance using voice commands.

AI-Driven Email Automation | AI enhances email marketing by optimizing subject lines, email body content, and sending times to increase open rates and conversions. Machine learning algorithms analyze user engagement with past email campaigns to determine the best approach for future communication.

As conversational AI becomes more advanced, businesses can create more natural, intuitive, and seamless customer interactions that enhance user satisfaction and brand engagement.

The Integration of AI with Augmented Reality (AR) and Virtual Reality (VR)

The fusion of AI, AR, and VR is transforming how businesses engage with their audiences by creating immersive and interactive digital experiences.

AI-Powered Virtual Shopping Assistants | AI-driven virtual assistants enhance online shopping by providing real-time recommendations, answering queries, and assisting customers in making informed purchasing decisions. These AI assistants simulate in-store shopping experiences by offering product suggestions based on browsing behavior.

AR-Based Product Visualization | Businesses leverage AR technology to allow customers to visualize products in real-world environments before making a purchase. AI enhances this experience by personalizing suggestions based on user preferences, ensuring a more tailored and satisfactory shopping experience.

Interactive AI-Driven Marketing Campaigns | Brands use AR and VR technology to create engaging marketing campaigns that encourage user interaction. AI customizes these experiences based on audience demographics and behavior, making them more effective in capturing attention and driving conversions.

By integrating AI with AR and VR, businesses can craft immersive experiences that deepen customer engagement and influence purchasing decisions.

AI and Voice Search Optimization

With the growing popularity of voice search, AI is playing a crucial role in ensuring businesses optimize their content for voice-based queries.

Natural Language Processing (NLP) for Understanding Search Intent | AI-powered NLP helps brands understand the nuances of spoken queries, allowing them to tailor content accordingly. This ensures that businesses appear in relevant voice search results by adapting their SEO strategies to voice-based search patterns.

Structuring Website Content for Voice Search | AI helps reformat website content to align with conversational search patterns. This includes optimizing for question-based queries and structuring information to provide direct, concise answers.

Enhancing Local SEO Strategies for Voice Search Users | Many voice searches are local-based, such as users looking for nearby services. AI assists businesses in optimizing their content and listings for local SEO, increasing visibility for users searching via voice commands.

As voice search adoption continues to grow, businesses that leverage AI to optimize their content will benefit from increased discoverability and engagement.

AI-Enhanced Advertising and Media Buying

AI is redefining how businesses approach advertising and media buying by optimizing ad placements, targeting, and content in real-time.

AI-Driven Programmatic Advertising | AI automates media buying by identifying the most suitable audience segments and placing ads accordingly. This ensures that marketing budgets are used efficiently, reducing costs and improving return on investment (ROI).

Dynamic Ad Creatives Adjusted for Audience Engagement | AI enables advertisers to personalize ad content dynamically based on user interactions. This approach ensures that audiences receive the most relevant and engaging ads tailored to their preferences.

Predictive Models for Campaign Effectiveness | AI-generated models assess historical advertising data to predict which campaigns will perform best. Businesses use these insights to optimize ad spend, refine targeting strategies, and improve overall campaign effectiveness.

With AI's ability to analyze vast amounts of data in real-time, businesses can refine their advertising strategies, leading to more effective and cost-efficient marketing campaigns.

Ethical AI and Data Privacy in Marketing

As AI becomes increasingly integrated into marketing strategies, ethical concerns and data privacy considerations must be addressed.

Transparency in AI Decision-Making Processes | Companies must ensure that AI-driven marketing strategies are transparent, allowing consumers to understand how their data is being used. Implementing ethical guidelines for AI usage can help build trust and improve customer relationships.

Adherence to Data Privacy Regulations | Businesses must comply with data protection laws such as GDPR and CCPA. AI-driven marketing solutions should be designed to protect user privacy, ensuring compliance with legal standards and best practices.

Developing Responsible AI Systems | Ethical AI development involves creating algorithms that avoid biases and ensure fairness in decision-making. Businesses should regularly audit their AI models to detect and mitigate potential biases that could impact marketing strategies.

By balancing AI innovation with ethical considerations, businesses can foster consumer trust while leveraging AI to improve marketing effectiveness.

Expanding these aspects allows businesses to better understand and implement AI-driven strategies while ensuring ethical responsibility and compliance.

THE FUTURE OF AI-POWERED AUTOMATION IN MARKETING

Automation continues to evolve, streamlining various marketing tasks. Future developments in AI-powered automation include:

Automated Content Creation

AI is set to play a crucial role in content generation, assisting brands in maintaining high-quality output that aligns with their messaging and tone. Businesses can leverage AI to:

- Generate written content for blogs, social media, and email marketing.
- Enhance visual content creation, including graphics and video automation.
- Optimize content for SEO by analyzing search trends and keyword performance.
- Personalize content for different audience segments based on engagement data.

By integrating AI into content creation processes, brands can ensure consistency and relevance while reducing the manual workload for marketers.

Dynamic Pricing Strategies

AI-powered pricing models enable businesses to adjust their prices in real-time based on multiple factors, such as:

- Consumer demand fluctuations.
- Competitor pricing strategies.
- Market trends and seasonal influences.
- Customer purchase history and willingness to pay.

These strategies help businesses remain competitive while maximizing profitability. AI-powered pricing tools can also test various pricing strategies to determine the most effective approaches for different customer segments.

Automated Sales Funnels

AI is reshaping how businesses approach lead nurturing and conversion optimization through:

- AI-driven lead scoring to prioritize high-potential customers.
- Automated email sequences that respond to user interactions.
- Chatbots and conversational AI guiding prospects through the sales funnel.
- Predictive analytics to identify the best moments for engagement.

With AI-driven automation, businesses can build more efficient, scalable sales funnels that cater to individual customer needs.

AI-Powered CRM Integration

Customer relationship management (CRM) systems are becoming more intelligent with AI integration. Businesses can use AI-enhanced CRM systems to:

- Analyze customer interactions and predict future behaviors.
- Provide personalized recommendations for sales and marketing teams.
- Automate follow-up communications and reminders.
- Detect patterns in customer data to improve engagement strategies.

AI-powered CRM tools offer businesses valuable insights that lead to better customer relationships and more informed decision-making.

By embracing AI-driven automation in these areas, businesses can operate more efficiently and deliver enhanced customer experiences, positioning themselves for sustained growth in an increasingly digital landscape.

CHALLENGES AND CONSIDERATIONS FOR THE FUTURE

Balancing AI Automation with Human Creativity

AI has made it possible to automate many aspects of marketing, from content generation to customer service. However, human creativity remains indispensable in crafting compelling brand narratives, ensuring authenticity, and making strategic decisions that align with broader business goals.

Maintaining Brand Authenticity and Storytelling | AI-generated content can be efficient, but it often lacks the emotional depth and originality that human creativity brings. Businesses must strike a balance by leveraging AI for efficiency while ensuring human oversight to maintain authenticity.

Aligning AI-Generated Content with Marketing Objectives | While AI tools can generate high-quality content, businesses should ensure it aligns with their core messaging and brand identity. Human marketers should fine-tune AI outputs to enhance consistency and relevance.

Using AI Insights to Complement Human-Driven Strategies | AI excels in analyzing data and predicting trends, but human judgment is necessary to contextualize insights and apply them creatively. By integrating AI-driven analytics with human expertise, businesses can refine their marketing strategies while maintaining a unique brand voice.

AI Bias and Ethical Considerations

AI models rely on historical data, which may include biases that can inadvertently affect decision-making. Businesses must be proactive in addressing these ethical concerns to maintain fairness and inclusivity.

Auditing AI-Driven Processes for Fairness and Inclusivity | Regular audits of AI algorithms can help identify and mitigate biases. Businesses should invest in unbiased training data and ethical AI development practices to ensure equitable marketing outcomes.

Implementing Ethical AI Frameworks to Guide Marketing Decisions | Establishing clear guidelines for AI use in marketing can help businesses ensure ethical practices. These frameworks should prioritize fairness, transparency, and accountability in AI-driven decision-making.

Maintaining Transparency in AI-Driven Marketing Strategies | Transparency in how AI tools analyze and use consumer data is essential for building trust. Businesses should communicate how AI is used in marketing and provide consumers with clear options to control their data.

Data Privacy and Regulatory Compliance

As AI-driven marketing tools become more advanced, ensuring data security and compliance with regulations is crucial. Businesses must take proactive measures to protect customer data and adhere to legal requirements.

Adhering to Privacy Laws Such as GDPR and CCPA | Compliance with regulations is essential for businesses using AI in marketing. Organizations should stay informed about evolving data privacy laws and implement necessary compliance measures.

Providing Customers with Control Over Their Data | Consumers are increasingly concerned about how their data is collected and used. Businesses should offer transparent data policies and allow users to manage their preferences regarding data collection and usage.

Strengthening Cybersecurity Measures to Protect Sensitive Information | AI-driven marketing relies on vast amounts of consumer data, making cybersecurity a top priority. Organizations should implement strong encryption, secure data storage solutions, and regular security audits to safeguard customer information.

Evolving AI Technology and Adaptation Challenges

AI technology is advancing rapidly, requiring businesses to stay agile and adapt to new developments. Successful integration of AI into marketing strategies depends on ongoing learning and flexibility.

Staying Updated on AI Advancements and Best Practices | The landscape of AI in marketing is constantly evolving. Businesses should actively monitor new AI trends, attend industry conferences, and invest in research to stay ahead of technological shifts.

Training Marketing Teams to Effectively Use AI-Powered Tools | Adoption of AI requires a workforce that understands how to utilize AI tools effectively. Organizations should provide training programs to equip marketing teams with the knowledge and skills needed to leverage AI efficiently.

Ensuring AI Integrations Align with Long-Term Business Goals | While AI offers numerous benefits, it is important to integrate it strategically. Businesses should assess how AI-driven solutions align with their overall business objectives and customer needs, ensuring a seamless transition and meaningful impact.

By addressing these challenges thoughtfully, businesses can harness AI's potential while maintaining ethical standards, regulatory compliance, and a strong connection with their audience.

FUTURE OPPORTUNITIES FOR AI IN DIGITAL MARKETING

Despite challenges, AI presents numerous opportunities for marketers. Areas of future innovation include:

AI-Powered Influencer Marketing

AI is transforming influencer marketing by helping brands identify, evaluate, and collaborate with influencers more effectively. Machine learning algorithms analyze engagement rates, audience demographics, and content quality to determine the best partnerships. AI-powered tools can assess an influencer's credibility by detecting fake followers and engagement manipulation, ensuring brands invest in authentic collaborations. Additionally, AI can optimize influencer campaign strategies by predicting content performance and suggesting adjustments in real-time.

Brands also use AI to automate influencer outreach and relationship management, allowing for more scalable and efficient collaborations. By integrating AI-driven insights, marketers can enhance influencer selection, track campaign effectiveness, and refine engagement strategies based on data-driven metrics.

Automated Emotional AI

AI-driven sentiment analysis is refining brand messaging by assessing consumer emotions in text, voice, and visual content. Businesses can use Natural Language Processing (NLP) to analyze customer feedback, social media posts, and online reviews, gaining insights into audience perceptions and reactions.

Automated emotional AI enables brands to craft marketing messages that resonate with their audience, adjusting tone and language based on sentiment analysis. This helps brands tailor their communication strategies to foster stronger connections with consumers. AI-driven chatbots and virtual assistants also use sentiment analysis to provide more empathetic and personalized customer interactions.

Furthermore, emotional AI enhances advertising strategies by evaluating consumer reactions to visual and video content. Brands can modify ad creatives in real-time based on emotional responses, ensuring more engaging and effective marketing campaigns.

AI in Video Marketing

Video marketing is evolving with AI-powered tools that streamline video creation, editing, and performance tracking. AI assists in video production by automating scriptwriting, scene recommendations, and voiceovers. AI-based tools analyze video performance, providing data-driven insights on audience engagement, retention rates, and optimal video length.

Brands leverage AI-powered personalization to tailor video content to individual viewers. AI dynamically generates video variations based on user preferences, past interactions, and browsing behavior, making content more relevant and engaging.

Additionally, AI enhances video accessibility by generating automatic captions, translations, and audio descriptions. This broadens the reach of video content to a more diverse audience, including those with disabilities or language barriers.

Real-Time AI-Generated Market Insights

AI enables businesses to gain deeper consumer insights through real-time analytics. Machine learning algorithms process vast amounts of market data, detecting trends, consumer preferences, and emerging opportunities. AI-driven predictive analytics allow marketers to anticipate shifts in consumer behavior and adjust strategies accordingly.

Real-time AI-generated insights help businesses optimize ad placements, refine targeting strategies, and improve content relevance. AI-powered tools analyze social media conversations, news articles, and industry reports to provide brands with a comprehensive understanding of market dynamics.

By leveraging AI for market insights, businesses can make data-driven decisions faster, ensuring they stay ahead of competitors and respond to consumer needs with agility. AI's ability to process and interpret complex data sets enhances strategic planning and marketing effectiveness, leading to better customer engagement and business growth.

AI, marketing technology (MarTech), and automation are reshaping digital marketing by enhancing efficiency, personalization, and decision-making. These innovations enable businesses to refine targeting, streamline workflows, and engage with audiences in more meaningful ways. As AI capabilities continue to evolve, their role in predictive analytics, content creation, customer interactions, and marketing automation will expand, influencing the way brands connect with consumers.

Despite the advantages, businesses must navigate challenges such as data privacy, ethical AI use, and balancing automation with human creativity. Ensuring compliance with regulations, maintaining transparency in AI-driven processes, and integrating AI tools strategically will be key to responsible implementation.

Looking ahead, AI-driven influencer marketing, emotional AI, video automation, and real-time market insights will open new opportunities for businesses. Companies that stay adaptable, invest in AI education, and integrate automation with a customer-centric approach will be well-positioned to leverage AI's potential for long-term growth. As digital marketing continues to evolve, AI and automation will remain integral to creating more efficient, responsive, and data-driven marketing strategies.

Key Takeaways

- AI is reshaping digital marketing by improving efficiency, personalization, and automation.
- AI-driven tools enhance customer interactions, content generation, predictive analytics, and marketing automation.
- Emerging trends include hyper-personalization, conversational AI, AI-powered AR/VR experiences, and voice search optimization.
- AI-driven advertising optimizes media buying and dynamic ad content based on engagement data.
- Ethical considerations, including AI bias, data privacy, and transparency, remain essential for responsible AI adoption.
- Future opportunities include AI-powered influencer marketing, emotional AI, video marketing automation, and real-time consumer insights.

Reflection Questions

- How can your business integrate AI-driven personalization to enhance customer engagement?
- What aspects of your current marketing strategy could benefit from AI automation?
- Which emerging AI trends in marketing are most relevant to your industry?

Action Steps

- Identify AI-powered tools that align with your marketing objectives, such as chatbots, predictive analytics, or content automation.
- Update your website content to accommodate conversational search queries and structured data formats.
- Use AI to analyze customer behavior and refine marketing messages for a more tailored experience.
- Regularly audit AI-driven marketing processes to maintain GDPR and CCPA compliance.
- Establish internal guidelines for AI usage, ensuring transparency and fairness in AI-driven marketing decisions.
- Follow industry trends and advancements to maintain a competitive edge in AI adoption.

FINAL THOUGHTS
THE HUMAN TOUCH IN A DIGITAL WORLD

The integration of artificial intelligence, marketing technology, and automation is reshaping digital marketing, providing businesses with tools to enhance decision-making, streamline operations, and improve customer engagement. Throughout this book, we have explored how AI-powered MarTech supports data-driven strategies, enables personalization, and enhances efficiency in various marketing functions, from content creation and customer segmentation to predictive analytics and performance measurement.

While AI offers practical benefits, its adoption also comes with challenges. Ethical considerations, data privacy, and the importance of human oversight remain critical in ensuring responsible and effective implementation. Rather than replacing human expertise, AI should be seen as a tool that enhances strategic decision-making and operational efficiency. Striking a balance between automation and human judgment will be key to making the most of these technologies.

Looking ahead, the continued evolution of AI and MarTech will present new opportunities and considerations for marketers. Staying informed, adaptable, and critical in evaluating emerging technologies will help businesses integrate AI effectively while maintaining a focus on customer experience and long-term objectives. Those who approach AI with a clear strategy, grounded in both technological potential and practical constraints, will be better positioned to navigate an increasingly data-driven marketing environment.

As AI continues to evolve, its role in marketing will likely expand, offering new ways to analyze data, engage audiences, and optimize performance. Organizations that integrate these tools thoughtfully will be better equipped to adapt to changes in the digital landscape and refine their marketing strategies in meaningful ways.

ABOUT THE AUTHOR

Rohit Srivastava is a marketing professional with almost two decades of experience in leadership roles across diverse sectors where he developed a comprehensive understanding of marketing, branding, and business processes. He has spent years exploring the intersection of digital marketing and artificial intelligence, helping businesses navigate the fast-changing digital world. He has worked with startups, established brands, and tech-driven Fortune 500 companies, crafting AI-powered solutions that make marketing smarter, not harder.

Rohit holds an MBA in Information Technology and Marketing, along with multiple marketing certifications from top-tier institutions. His qualifications support his methodical approach to integrating technology into marketing practices. He has visited multiple countries to mentor and guide people in the core principles of digital brand building.

His background encompasses a wide range of marketing disciplines, from performance marketing and competitive analysis to marketing automation, digital strategy, and more.

Beyond work, Rohit loves traveling, reading, and spending time with his family. These interests help him stay balanced and open to new ideas, both professionally and personally.

He is committed to sharing knowledge that is both accessible and actionable, a commitment reflected in this book. If you're interested in learning more about him or connecting with him professionally, please visit his LinkedIn profile.

Want to stay connected?

LinkedIn: www.linkedin.com/in/rohitsrivastavas

Email: rohitkslko@gmail.com

www.ingramcontent.com/pod-product-compliance
Ingram Content Group UK Ltd.
Pitfield, Milton Keynes, MK11 3LW, UK
UKHW041348190726
13845UKWH00026B/497

9 789334 241488